RECLAIM YOUR VISIBILITY

A Straightforward Guide for Black Fathers to Improve Themselves and Their Relationships with Their Children

To Daniel,

I am so proud of your accomplishment. Keep elevating. I wrote this book for Black Fathers because I wrote it to my younger self.

However, the messages ring true no matter what your background is.

Stay Visible,
Carl Stokes
1-14-21

Dr. Carl Stokes Jr.

STOKESMEDIA LLC

Copyright © 2020 by Stokes Media, LLC

Cover Design: Tri Widyatmaka
Interior Design: Waqar Nadeem
Logo Design: Darrell Stevens
Editor: Jessica Sipos, PhD
Cover Photography: Naylani Arielle Stokes

All rights reserved. No part of this publication may be reproduced, used, performed, stored in a retrieval system, or transmitted in any form or by any means, electronic, mechanical, photocopying, recording or otherwise without the prior written permission of the author Dr. Carl Stokes Jr., except for critical articles and reviews.

For booking inquiries/bulk copy purchases visit:

www.drcarlstokesjr.com

1st edition, December 2020
ISBN – 13: 978-1-7359202-0-7
Printed in the United States of America

DEDICATION

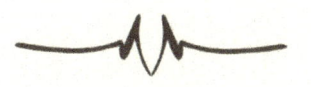

This book is dedicated to Black men. This book is dedicated to Black Fathers. This book is for progress for us as Black people. This book is for those of us who went without the love, support, and nurturing of a father, even when they were alive and well. This is for those of us who never knew how to show that love, support, and nurturing as a father. This book is for every Black child who ever had to wait around for their father who never came. This book is for the Black fathers who have children waiting for them right now.

TABLE OF CONTENTS

DEDICATION..3

INTRODUCTION......................................7

THE TWELVE "Ps"

STEP ONE: Take the **Pledge**..................14

STEP TWO: Take **Personal** Responsibility.........19

STEP THREE: Realize Your **Power**...................39

STEP FOUR: **Presence** Over Presents................50

STEP FIVE: Embrace **Pulchritude**......................60

STEP SIX: Stop Advertising Your **Problems**..... 70

STEP SEVEN: Keep Your **Promises**.................. 77

STEP EIGHT: **Practice** Self-Care 83

STEP NINE: Let Go of the **Past**.......................... 89

STEP TEN: Get Rid of **Pollution**........................ 99

STEP ELEVEN: Include the Right **People**........103

STEP TWELVE: **Plan** and Execute....................110

CONCLUSION...115

EXTRA STEP (Bonus):

Black Fathers in Jail and **Prison**..........................122

ACKNOWLEDGEMENTS............................... 127

INTRODUCTION

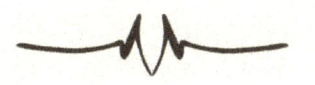

This book is for you, my brother. Yes, YOU! I'm so glad you are here. I am excited that you are taking an active role in your own self-development. With that mindset, you are already ahead of the game. This book is an honest, straight-to-the-point guide for Black fathers who are looking to be better men and looking to better their relationships with their children. We will go through 12 simple steps to help you get there. After we conclude, and you are ready to make things happen, I will provide you with specific examples of how I used these very steps during my own personal journey.

There is a disclaimer, though. Although this book is straight fire, it is not a magic pill or some sort of quick fix. You have to do your part. If you are not looking to put in the work, stop here because this isn't for you. If you are already approaching this with a closed mind, this isn't for you. Most importantly, if improving your relationship(s) with your child(ren) is not a priority, then this is *definitely* not for you. You can get off right here.

Those of you who are ready to embark on this journey, let's make it happen!

Also, for the haters (because even when you try to do something good, there are always haters!), the approach and delivery of this book is intentional. I am who I am, I'm from where I'm from, and I'm proud of it. This book is written in *my* voice. But just for context, I received my associate degree in social science from Erie Community College in Buffalo, New York, my bachelor degree in sociology from Buffalo State College, my master of social work degree from the University of Buffalo, my social work license from the New York State Department of Education, and my doctorate in education from St. John Fisher College in Rochester, New York. Do not play with me.

I put this system in place through the best way I learn: trial and error. So, trust me when I say that I made A LOT of mistakes during my Black fatherhood journey. I made errors so plentiful and as egregious as a father that it would be a criminal act of negligence against the Black community if I didn't attempt to help as many people as I could now! I am not saying I have all the answers, but I definitely have some. My intention is to present these steps in a way that there is something in them for each Black father regardless of circumstance. Whether you are really struggling or doing well, whatever your relationship status is, this book has some relatability. Like I said, it's for you.

In addition to you, this book is also for your wonderful son, your beautiful daughter, or both. This book is intended to benefit you directly, and thereby your child(ren) indirectly. However, I suppose it's only fair that I recognize the fact that helping you and the little ones also benefits that lovely wife or girlfriend of yours. Or perhaps it can benefit that ex that you can't seem to get along with!

Even better, maybe you have an ex you *do* get along with. Or you could be like me and have not even an iota of a relationship with the mother of your child or children. What?!?! That's right. Mr.-fancy Dr.-author social worker /father / husband / uncle / brother-Stokes probably is, or at least has been, a worse father than you for a period of time in his life. It is certainly not something I'm proud of, and it is definitely not a competition. I'm not happy to have the intercontinental championship title for bad fatherhood practices. However, I present my chief flaw as a promise of transparency to you. Yes, YOU!

Trust me, if I can find a way to reclaim my visibility as a Black father, you my friend, are in good shape. We call it reclaiming our visibility because Black fathers are often invisible. We are unseen. We are not seen in many households with our children.

We are not seen when it comes to decision making. We are not thought about when it comes to our children's schools. Here is the thing, though. Sometimes it's our own fault. Fortunately, I happen to be on the upswing as I have made leaps and bounds as a man. Although I have worked hard to become an exceptional father, I still struggle with my past mistakes, attitude, and overall mentality.

I had my first child at a very young age, well before I was ready. I didn't even know who I was yet. Unfortunately, when I did find out who I was, I didn't like him at all. I know you may feel the same way. People didn't know my struggle and I know some of the people close to you don't know yours. Without exaggeration, it took me close to 20 years to love myself again. If not for reclaiming my visibility, I would have fallen victim to the anger, depression, self-hate, doubt, and shame that I was living with. I set up shop in the darkest places of my mind and soul and got very comfortable with being uncomfortable. What I'm saying to you, my brother, is that I understand, and I swear on everything I love, I feel your pain.

Do you know what the original title of this book was called? Third Generation Deadbeat. When I told people the title they instantly got turned off. They said, "Why would anybody want to read that?" It came across as if I was bragging about being a terrible father. When I shared it with one of the premier mental health/substance abuse professionals in Western New York, André Stokes (my younger brother), he said "Why the f@#k would anybody want to read that?" Damn son, ouch! It's not that he didn't want to read it, it just neglected to talk about the comeback I had from being a lackluster version of the father I am, to the proud person and father that I stand as today. That original title just flat out said that I was a bad father and left it there as if that was the end of my story.

See, the premise of Third Generation Deadbeat was that my late father, Carl Stokes Sr. was by definition, a deadbeat dad. He was an extraordinary person, but he was one of the many Black men in America who fell victim to the crack epidemic in the 1980s. I mean, the dude was one of the coolest, most charismatic people ever. You know those types of people that everybody just gravitates towards? That was him. Unfortunately, his lack of presence in me and André's lives was largely due to his addiction.

Now, his father was also a deadbeat dad. He moved down south somewhere and didn't have much to do with my father throughout his life. I never even met the dude. So, after seeing all the historic fatherlessness in my lineage, I vowed that I would never be that way when I became a father. I decided at a young age that I was not going to do drugs like my father, and I certainly would not move away from my child when I had one like my grandfather. The crazy thing is, as adamant as I was that it would never happen, I somehow became that same deadbeat dad. Three generations in, as if I was genetically predisposed to it. Just to think, because I never knew my grandfather, I have no knowledge of his father, or the one before that. This means the trend could go back four or more generations. That's scary to think about.

Another notch in the negative stereotypical belt of Black Fatherhood, and I had the dubious honor of being a contributing member. What was the prize? I received an all-expense paid trip to shame, pain, hopelessness, embarrassment, and despair. If you are in any of those places, I'm here to help to get you out. If you are headed to one of those places, I am here to help redirect you. If you are far away from those places, I will meet you where you are and help to keep you occupied so you stay away. Keep in mind the key word is *help*. This is your journey. I'm just a tour guide.

As the title of this book suggests, I had to reclaim my visibility because I was missing. I was absent. I was not recognized. I was overlooked. I had a baby in high school with the first girl I ever had sex with. I had no idea what I was doing, what I was going to do, and *I had nobody to teach me anything*. I had a difficult time navigating and it cost me dearly. It cost me my relationship with my first-born child. It cost me my mental health, my joy, my spirit, my confidence, and my overall well-being. It forced me to distance myself from good people, and made it easy to surround myself with destructive ones. I went through hell and back multiple times over until I changed to become the man you see on the cover of this book.

My purpose is to do my best to help you get here with me. Remember, I said help. It's a great place to be. I want to see you get over your struggles. I want to see you get over your bad decisions and your perceived bad luck. I want to see you find yourself again, or find yourself for the first time. I want to see you love yourself and accept the fact that you can and will reclaim what's rightfully yours . . . your visibility. Yes, YOU! This book is short by design because I want you to get through and not have it laying around unfinished. Let's knock this one out for the cause, big man. You got this. This is light work!

Oh yeah, you will find lyrics quoted from various hip-hop artists that correspond with each step as a reminder of the power of influence in our music.

STEP ONE

TAKE THE PLEDGE

Love, knowledge and discipline too/I pledge my life to you

- Will Smith *"Just the Two of Us"*

Before you go any further, I want you to ask yourself why you are reading this book. I'm talking about in the most basic sense. Why did you even pick it up? Why did you open it? Are you reading it to mend your relationship with your child(ren)? Are you looking to establish a relationship that has failed to materialize? Are you just looking to get better as a father? Do you need to feel heard? Well, I hear you. We hear you. Let's make sure that we gain something from taking this journey together. I'm saying "we" because I want you to think about me reading this right along with you. I want you to also think about all the Black fathers who are reading this along with you as well. Page by page. Together.

Stereotypes suggest that Black people, especially us Black men don't stick together. That's funny because we're often stuck together. Stuck in a rut. Stuck in a world where we are falsely accused, judged, ridiculed, and feared. Stuck being aggravated. Stuck not knowing what to do, and stuck dreaming about being where we want to be in life. But all it takes is a first step in combating the stereotype of our inability to move as a cohesive unit. Let's make our first step together be the Black Fatherhood Pledge.

A pledge is a promise. Remember when you had to do the Pledge of Allegiance in school every day? Before you started the day, every single day, you and the rest of your class stood up, faced the American flag in the classroom, put your right hand over your heart, and said the pledge. You probably don't even remember learning it. It's as if it was always there stored in your memory. As you're reading this, I bet you can recite that pledge without missing a word!

So, let's do *this* pledge for us. The Pledge of Allegiance was to promise your loyalty to the country. The World Wildlife Fund has the Pledge for Our Planet. The National Safety Council has the Safe at Work Pledge. Let's hit them with our Black Fatherhood Pledge.

Put that almighty Black fist of yours over your heart. If you are alone, think about all of your brothers who, like you, want to be better people, better men, and better fathers. If you are physically in a room with other brothers reading this together, feel their energy along with yours and say the following pledge in unison:

THE BLACK FATHERHOOD PLEDGE

"I pledge to give my all to my child(ren) in the spirit of Black Fatherhood. In order to do so, I will first work to improve myself. I accept the damage that I may have caused, and I forgive myself. I accept the damage that others may have caused, and I forgive them. I will not rest until I make things right. I will not place blame on anybody else, especially my child(ren) for my situation. I love myself. I love my child(ren). Today, I will reclaim my visibility"

Congratulations my good brother. You have just dispelled one of the many Black male stereotypes that has plagued our community for years. You and other brothers just like yourself have worked to find a commonality. You have worked to find a purpose. You have worked to find a way to stick together.

Let's do this.

STEP ONE TAKEAWAYS

1. The fact that you have chosen to engage with this book means are in the right state of mind. Be proud of that.
2. Taking the Black Fatherhood Pledge is preparation for your journey.
3. This is bonding with the rest of the like-minded Black fathers with the same goal.

ACTIONS TO TAKE

1. Make the pledge to yourself.
2. Go to drcarlstokesjr.com and print out a copy of the pledge.
3. Sign the pledge, and post it on the door, wall, window, or mirror.
4. Read it aloud to yourself every day.

STEP TWO

TAKE PERSONAL RESPONSIBILITY

If you're not moving ahead you, you're bugging/you got to look at yourself and try to change something - KRS-One "Break the Chain"

Embrace your status as a Black man. Scratch that. Embrace your status as a STRONG Black man. Realize and understand that. Can you feel it? I know I certainly can. It is because I can feel your strength and resilience that I am going to talk to you openly and honestly. In other words, I know you can take it! Some might consider it harsh. Some will consider it just keeping it real. I'm talking to you as your brother. Your friend. Your contact from the future that needs you to take my word for what I have to say. In the movie Back to the Future Part II, old Biff went back in time to visit his young self. He brought a sports almanac from the future with all the scores of the games and convinced his young self to take it and place bets to become rich. Think of me as Biff, just Black, way cooler and using my power from the future to do good for my brothers as opposed to being greedy. Take my "almanac" and check the scores. Use my shortcomings to minimize opportunities for yours. Use my successes to be more successful than me. Take the good parts of my journey and learn from the bad ones. Its tough love, and I promise I got love for you.

But...

Do everybody a favor and get over yourself. The day you signed up to be a father, it should have stopped being all about you. I don't care if it was planned or not. The children should be, or should have been the priority in your life. I'm talking about right from the jump, dude. What the young boys say out here? *No cap!* Whether you were in love, thought that you may have been in love, or was just messing around with some chick you didn't vet properly, it doesn't matter at this point. The little ones are here now. Stop whining and complaining. Stop dwelling on what you could have had, what you should have had, what "your mans" has, or whatever else you are feeling sorry for yourself about. Nobody wants to hear it. You're like the Black male version of Debbie Downer from Saturday Night Live. You bring the energy in the room down with all of that.

Taking personal responsibility for your actions not only benefits you, it benefits us as a people. If all of us Black men did that, we would be in a different state of existence. When a man can own up to his mistakes, he can correct them. When a man blames everybody else for his circumstances, he is saying that he is without flaws which is inaccurate, immature, and flat out insane. Pay attention to who the common denominator is in all your drama. If you put all your problems on everybody and everything else, you rob yourself of opportunities to grow. Even when somebody else in my circle makes things difficult for me, I blame myself for not recognizing the potential threat earlier. I also take responsibility for not being on a different level and having to associate with said person. If I get shortchanged because of somebody who doesn't have their stuff together, shame on me for being within their reach. That's real.

See, your problem is that you let that volatile relationship between you and the kids' mother(s) dictate your relationship with the kids. There is no way that type of arrangement should take place, especially as some sort of twisted default setting. I know, I know. She doesn't help you with the relationship with the kids. She doesn't promote you as a father. She bad mouths you around them. She emasculates you. She worships the next dude and your children think he is the GOAT. You're jealous. Maybe he *is* the goat. Maybe him holding the household down is making you feel insecure about your station in life. Hey, I have been there. I know what it's like to have good traits, but at the same time feel like its wasted currency. I used to say to myself, "Everybody loves me except the people who are supposed to love me." You might be the most popular guy in the room, in rooms that your children are not in, and that hurts.

I am going to tell you what I wish somebody would have told me when I was in your position. Hear me clearly. I understand that men's brains are not fully developed until the age of 25, but you are a child yourself. Yeah, I said it. You are a child with children. I can say that because I was a child well after my childhood years. I needed to be a man and you need to be one too. A man does not whine and complain. A man does not throw temper tantrums. A man does not need to talk about how big and bad he is. A man does not hate another man's success. He knows damn well there's enough success to go around. A man does not have "beef" with another man because he now has the spot you lost with the woman and children.

See, there is chronological and developmental age. Chronological age is the actual number of years you are. Developmental age is the level of functionality or maturity at which you operate. In other words, you could be 26 years old chronologically, but 11 years old developmentally. Does your chronological age line up with your developmental age? Do your actions truly support your answer? You cannot lie to yourself. When you are done reading this book, go and listen to verse 2 of "Second Childhood" on the Nas album *Stillmatic*. Not to say this is you, but just to get an example of what I mean.

On everything I love, I believed that my first-born child got a tainted picture of who I was. I could never verify it, but it seemed likely. It seemed likely that I was talked about negatively, dragged through the mud, discredited, and so on. On top of that, I felt that any good qualities I possessed were completely overlooked. Mind you, I *fel*t like that was going on, but I never knew for sure. Either way, what did I do to combat it? I'll tell you what I did - a whole bunch of nothing. Therefore, I played right into it. Again, I cannot verify that I was being dragged, but it doesn't matter. If I was being slandered, I proved the statements right and gave people the ammunition to make the statements. If I wasn't being slandered, then I actively participated in discrediting myself.

Either way, I played into it by standing by, watching and letting it take place. For years I did this. Don't be like me. I used avoidance as my game plan. Does that sound like a successful game plan? Think about all the problems you "handled" by not handling them.

However, I justified it by telling myself that I had to "fall back" or else I would flip out and cause trouble for myself. Can you believe that? I used the words "fall" and "back" about my position with my own child. If I had a time machine, I would set it to the date I said that, go there and punch that logic right out of my own face! Straight up.

Listen brother, don't do superficial things instead of substantive things. I paid for sneakers when I should have paid attention. What do you do to combat your suspicion that you are being discredited as a father? Do you watch movies? Scroll through social media for hours? Do you read to your children? Oh, you don't live there anymore. Well, do you set up online meetings with your children? No? That's interesting because you stay Facetiming those jump-offs that you meet on hookup sites. You're doing all kinds of Skyping and video chatting with your boys about who got that "loud" or who is "getting it in." Why aren't you "getting it in" as it pertains to quality time and asking how your child's day was? You could simply call and say, "Hey, little man, Daddy just wanted to holler at you real fast. I wanted to know what your favorite part of the day was today." A little goes a long way brother. You'd be surprised at what kind of doors concern and consistency will open up for you.

Oh, wait, you *do* live there? Well, does it even count if you work all day and come home to scroll through social media and watch Kobe highlights on YouTube until you fall asleep while your son plays video games for five straight hours? Does it count if you are too busy and tried to tell your daughter how special she is? It better not be, because the first young boy who hits her with that line is going to have her at his mercy emotionally. You know the game. You've done it yourself. There is a misconception that girls without fathers in the home are always the wild ones. Anybody can be home in the physical sense. You need to be there emotionally. Stop letting Netflix, Hulu, Amazon and whatever other platforms raise your children. Or better yet, stop letting those things distract *you* from raising your children.

So, this is typically the point where I get a lot of fallout or people start getting really upset with me. However, I did say from the beginning that this was a straightforward guide. That was just my polite way of saying that I don't care! What needs to be said will be said. This is where the defenses are things like, "You don't know my situation," or "I've been doing all those things," or "You can't put that on us because Black men are in this predicament because of racism and years of oppression," or my personal favorite, "My father wasn't around, so I wasn't taught how to be one." Let's unpack these responses, shall we?

1. *You don't know my situation:* No, I don't. What I *do* know is that you have another level. My miracle scenario is as follows: You found out that you were the heir to a long-lost relative's fortune of $3.5 million. The will states that to receive the inheritance you need to level up. You need to finish school, start that business, stop smoking so you can pass drug tests to get a better job, and spend time with your children every day. Would you be able to level up? If your answer is yes, then that debunks your excuses. It also means that you will step up your game for money and not for yourself or your children. Think about that for a minute. If your answer is no, then you don't have the drive or determination and you don't really want to better your situation. You might as well stop reading this and go back to playing video games or getting "day drunk," or whatever you're doing that's preventing you from making progress.

2. *I've been doing all those things:* So? Do them better? Do them more often. Do those things, plus some new things. While this book is a guide, I understand that everybody's situation is different. You know your situation better than me, or anybody else. Only you can adapt to the nuances of your circumstances. You go to the car lot and buy a nice SUV because you have always wanted one. You drive it home and change the mats, the steering wheel cover, the music settings, the seat adjustment, the mirrors, and the air fresheners. You make it fit your lifestyle, your personality, your situation. No different here. Man up and make it work.

3. *You can't put that on us because Black men are in this predicament because of years of racism and oppression:* I understand history. I am a Black man in America just like you. In fact, I happen to be a scholar in the subject. I also happen to be a descendant of enslaved people. Your perception of what the "white man" has done to you has absolutely nothing to do with you loving your kids. It has nothing to do with you spending time with your kids. It has nothing to do with you calling your kids. I wouldn't even fix my mouth to say some nonsense like that.

As a matter of fact, I would argue that you should go even harder for your kids because of that history. On top of being brutalized themselves, your ancestors had to endure their children being overworked, beaten, raped, sold, and stripped right from their arms. They couldn't do anything about their circumstances. You can do something about yours. Yet, here you are using the history and plight of Black people as an excuse to give up on your children. I would consider that to be pretty insulting. What would the ancestors think? Stop bringing up white people. This is not about them; this is about us.

4. My father wasn't around, so I wasn't taught how to be one: There was also a time when you didn't know how to read. You didn't know how to count. You didn't know how to tell time. You didn't know how to drive. You didn't know how to dribble a basketball. You didn't know how to throw a football. You didn't know how to change a tire. You didn't know how to play an instrument. You didn't know how to draw. You didn't know how to talk to girls.

You didn't know the first thing about applying for a job. You didn't know how to apply for school. You didn't know how to register for classes. You didn't know how to open a bank account. You didn't know how to write a check. You didn't know how to start a business. You didn't know how to put up drywall.

As you can see, I can clearly fill up the rest of this book with examples, but I think you get it. Did your father teach you those things? Maybe he taught you none, maybe he taught you some, and maybe he taught you all of them. Did you learn the rest of the things on that list that apply to you? You most certainly did. You may have taught yourself. You may have been taught by a friend, relative, pastor, coach, teacher, neighbor, or whoever. The point is that you learned it. It may have been challenging, but you learned it. How is fatherhood any different? Even the best fathers make mistakes. Even the best fathers still learn and grow.

It's not a program that you can download once and everything is there. You have to be in to win it.

I have even heard people go as far as to say that their family is cursed. That is quite possibly the dumbest thing I ever heard. Let me explain to you how dangerous that type of thinking is. When you and your family members say that what you are doing is welcoming continued idiotic behavior and bad decision making.

If you say that your family is cursed to be poor, you are really just giving yourself permission to refrain from working hard, saving, investing, learning about finance, and making responsible decisions. You do that just so you can screw up, not pay your bills, constantly get evicted and hop from place to place to the point where your kids have no stability. But it's all good because you can just say, "See? That's the family curse." So, if your family "curse" is that fathers don't stick around, you should probably look to break the "curse" as opposed to falling into a self-fulfilling prophecy. I've heard it all. Can you believe that there are people that say they're cursed because sexual abuse of children continues to repeat generation after generation? However, instead of confronting the obvious behaviors, actors, and lack of adequate supervision, they allow the "curse" to take effect and continue to put the babies at risk. Sickening. That is nothing more than learned helplessness. That is when we repeatedly deal with negative situations, get frustrated, and then stop trying to change our circumstances, even though we have the ability to do so. Get out of here with that.

My research on Black fathers found that those who did not have fathers around were just as likely, or even more likely, to work hard at being fathers. The simple reason: so their children wouldn't have to go through the struggles of missing, wanting, or being depressed over not having their father around like they did. That is a terrible reason to not go hard for your little ones, my brother. Get it together.

When I teach classes, I speak about conflict. There are four main approaches to dealing with conflict. You can use avoidance, accommodation, aggression, and collaboration. As mentioned before, avoidance is just straight up not dealing with the issue. Let's look at it in the context of your relationship with the mother(s) of your children.

Avoidance. If you have issues that need to be discussed and you ignore them, the issues stick around. Not only do they stick around, they get worse. When you have suspicions of something not being right when it comes to the kids, address it. Your hunch is probably correct. Hell, even if you don't have suspicions, you need to check and follow up anyway. Sometimes we avoid things that we know we should address so we don't have to deal with the disruption to our lives. But you have to understand that there are some foul people out here, especially when it comes to kids. If you don't live in that house, you are not there to see the ins and outs, literally and figuratively. Follow this sentence carefully: ***People have a bad habit of trusting people without considering the trustworthiness of the people that the people they trust, trust.*** Let me break that down for you.

Be careful who you trust. Understanding trust is of the utmost importance. Especially when your babies are involved. Here is an example:

You trust your man Will with holding your grandfather's watch. He is a good dude, to you. You have known him your whole life. Now, Will trusts Reggie. He is a good dude, to Will. Will has known him his whole life. But see, you don't know Reggie. Reggie also doesn't know you. You let will hold the watch, but in doing that you have also given Reggie access to it. As much as you trust Will, he may unsuspectingly leave your watch vulnerable because his guard is down since he trusts Reggie. Pay attention and read between the lines and understand what I am saying to you as it pertains to your children.

Nobody is going to protect that "watch" the way you would. Get it? My kids hate me sometimes because I don't allow them to spend the night out at friend's houses. It's so funny how mad they get and how little I care about it! I tell the parents straight like this, "I know this is probably going to come off the wrong way, but your child can stay the night at our house any time, but my child is not allowed to stay the night out anywhere." They can take it or leave it. It's non-negotiable. Some parents get it, and some do not. So be it. If a parent told me that, we would probably become good friends because it would mean that they get it.

Take this situation, for example. I had a neighbor across the street when my daughter was about 7 or 8 years old. We lived directly across the street from one another. He was cool. His kids would come over to do homework with my daughter and my daughter would go over there some days. One cold Buffalo winter day, I had a meeting and was working late. My phone kept ringing and I silenced it quite a few times. It kept ringing though, so I had to excuse myself and answer it. It was the little girl from across the street, "Hi, Mr. Carl, this is (we'll call her) Tracy." I was confused and said, "Hi, Tracy, is everything okay?" She said, "My dad wanted me to call you because nobody was at the bus stop when we got off the bus, so your daughter is on our porch. My dad wants to know if she can come into the house."

Two letters for you to describe my neighbor, O.G.! White dude, by the way. Even though my daughter and his kids were friends, even though we were neighbors, even though my daughter has been in his house numerous times, even though his kids have been to my house numerous time, even though my wife and I had a miscommunication about bus duty, and even though it was freezing cold in the winter in Buffalo, New York, that man knew to get my permission before he let my little girl in his house. I would have done the same thing. Not too many people have that level of understanding.

You are a father. A protector. You need to recognize danger, or potential danger. If you sense that your child is experiencing something unpleasant, or feeling unsafe, how dare you avoid that? Your presence needs to be felt. People are predatory. They look for access and weak spots. An absent father is the biggest weak spot there is. You might as well have your kids wear a target on their backs every day. You might as well distribute flyers in the community announcing to predators that they can have free lunch at your ex-wife or baby's mother's house because there is no protector there. You, my friend, are an accessory if something happens to those kids. If the overnight security guard is asleep, or not in the building because he is avoiding his duties, and the place gets robbed, it's on him. If you are actively avoiding your children and something happens, I hope you can live with that, because your kids will have to.

A father who doesn't communicate regularly with his child and may not learn about something until it is too late is a weak spot. A child who doesn't have a relationship with their father is a weak spot. The problem is, the weak spot is not yours, and it's the child's. If you don't listen to anything else in this book listen to this. Be on it. It's not worth the risk. Be involved. Be a pain. Be annoying, inquisitive, and paranoid. Do not practice avoidance when it comes to your child. Err on the side of caution. Always. It is better to address things and find that there is no problem than to not address it and find out there is one. If a kid is getting bullied at school and deals with it by always running away, sneaking out of school, or ducking the bully at lunch time, then the problem will continue to exist and get worse.

Accommodation is another approach to conflict. It is basically settling. Now, it is okay to accommodate in certain situations. For example, your favorite restaurant makes accommodations for you. The nice resort in the Caribbean has beautiful accommodations. A place of employment needs to make reasonable accommodations for someone with impairments. You can make accommodations if it is healthy. Just look at it from a risk versus reward perspective.

Let's say you were supposed to pick up the kids, and their mother is not home at the designated time. You call her and tell her that you are in front of the house. She tells you that she is still at her mother's house way across town. You could either get into a huge argument, drive up your blood pressure, maybe get into an accident, or probably not see your kids. Or you could make the accommodations to drive to her mother's house and spend needed time with your kids.

Now if every time you have made arrangements this happens; you may need to make other arrangements. That would be accommodating to the point where it can become unproductive. That would be like the kid flat out giving the bully the lunch money he is after. Again, the problem will continue to exist or get worse.

Aggression as an approach to conflict is interesting. You have to be careful with it. First of all, there are two types of aggression. You have direct aggression and indirect (passive) aggression. Direct aggression is right in your face. It can be categorized as hostile or violent behavior, which does not work out for us Black men so well in family disputes. But it can also be looked at as overly assertive, which we can finesse to make things happen for us. For example, we can get aggressive with paying our bills. We can get aggressive with getting out of debt. We can get aggressive about saving money to buy a house. We can get aggressive in our pursuit of happiness. You are getting aggressive with making progress as a father by reading this book. Get aggressive with your desire to be father of the year, every year. This type of aggression is hunger. Get hungry. Get hyped. Being a father is the best job you will ever have. Appreciate it. Think about it. Nobody else can take your spot. I don't care about who is playing the role. YOU are the biological father. If not biological, YOU are the only real father that child has known. There is no other and can be no other. Hold your position and do it with pride.

The indirect or passive aggressiveness is the weak stuff. That doesn't suit us. That is the sneak dissing and being shady in a way where you act like it's unintentional. You know, giving somebody the silent treatment, or a negative vibe, but when they question you, you're like, "What?! No! I'm not trying to be…." Yeah, that's not a good look for you bro. Don't do that.

Collaboration as an approach to conflict is simply working together to complete a common goal. The common goal in your case is the child(ren) you created together. Even if you and their mother have a hard time getting along or seeing eye to eye, you have to be willing to work together for the sake of the kids, man. I know it can be difficult, but you have to elevate your mind and think beyond all the short-term stuff.

You are playing the long game here. If you need to find a mediator, do so. When I was in grad school, I did an internship with a human services agency that did supervised exchanges for parents who could not get along with each other. This is how it worked: The non-custodial parent (usually the dad) would come in at say, 1:00 pm, and debrief with the social worker about how things are going, what the plans for the visit are, and so on. The worker and the dad would be in the office until 1:15 pm. During that time, the custodial parent (usually the mom) would come in and drop off the children with another social worker, sign the papers, and leave. When the mom was well off the property, the social worker for the mom would call the social worker who was with dad to let him know the kids were there. Dad and the kids would then meet up and be free to go, with mom having a 15-minute head start. Some parents needed to do it that way because there would always be an issue at exchanges because they couldn't get past their disdain for each other for the sake of the children. If you have to employ new strategies, I encourage you to do so. The end result of that system was that the kids got to spend time with their dads. They didn't particularly enjoy having professional strangers in their business, and they certainly didn't enjoy sitting and sharing their issues with some intern, but they did what they had to do to be with their children.

STEP TWO TAKEAWAYS

1. You are stronger than you realize.

2. The tough love you receive from me is still love.

3. Taking personal responsibility empowers you to control what needs to be changed.

ACTIONS TO TAKE

1. Take a few minutes to do an honest audit of your role in your situation.

2. Write out a game plan or ideas that you come up with that can improve things.

3. Think about the approaches to conflict (Avoidance, Accommodation, Aggression, Collaboration) and make decisions on when and where to apply them.

STEP THREE

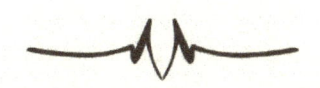

REALIZE YOUR POWER

The answers to all which are in front of me/The ultimate truth started to get blurry

- Speech "Tennessee"

Step Two was about taking personal responsibility on an individual level. Step Three is along the same lines, except that it is to be looked at in a more collective sense. What I mean is that we have to understand the power that we Black men have, especially when we move as one. We spend a lot of time asking for help when we could just help ourselves. Some of the issues that we have in our community have a snowball effect that brings an avalanche to wipe out our father-child relationships. There are a few things that we can do that we just let go to waste.

One is that we have the power to change the dynamics of Black love and relationships.

If we stopped degrading our own women, we could put ourselves in a much better position socially, economically, and politically in a short amount of time. What I mean is, if we treat our women better, we could help with keeping our families together. If we keep our families together, our children will have many benefits. If our children have those benefits of more stability, less chance of incarceration, more education, and less poverty, they can be more successful. I have been around for quite a while and I have yet to see other ethnic groups disparage their ladies the way we do. I mean, we don't even keep it in house. We let the whole world know that we don't respect our women. We publicly shame them in our everyday communication and in our music. Opportunists know we are an easy population to divide and conquer.

That's not how Black men should conduct themselves. Start recognizing how we are being trained, coerced, and hypnotized into thinking that disrespecting our queens is beneficial. We need to think and truly understand that these are the mothers of our children. Protect your Black women, brothers. Even when they be on that ridiculousness! We need to help them, not hurt them. Remember this, a lot of the nonsense that our women do, and the negative behaviors that they display, it's because of us, man. We treat them like crap in our romantic relationships, our sibling relationships, and our father-daughter relationships. Our women have had to first experience us as terrible fathers, which manifests into them acting out and hating us. Our daughters see us beating their mothers. They hear us belittle their mothers. Then they grow up to find another loser to take up with to replace us because they don't expect anything better. They do this instead of finding, or even wanting, somebody who has a good personality and a bright future.

We encourage Black women to be hood rats, complain about them acting as such, then wife them up anyway. We have the ability to change this by using our power for good instead of evil. If all of us Black men were ambitious, educated, loyal, responsible, kind, and sought out mates to complement those characteristics, we would have more negotiating power. In other words, if we improved ourselves and raised the bar, the caliber and quality of our women would improve. Is that what we want? No. We *say* that's what we want, but we look straight through the good ones and go straight for the ghetto, loud, gold-digging, and obnoxious, break your windows, slash your tires, run up and pop off at your job types of women. But the sex is off the chain, right? Then we have kids with them knowing damn well it's not going to work out. Then our relationships with our children suffer. Here is a little-known secret. Are you ready? You can use birth control and still do your thing without bringing children into your dysfunction.

Take that seriously because some of y'alls pull out game is hella weak!

Now, if we are not complaining about them being immature, it's about them being too rough. Too rough?! When they have been done wrong by us year after year, generation after generation, its called adaptability, son. They *need* to be rough and tough after going through what we put them through. There is nothing more ridiculous than a Black man who wears tight pants, gossips, wears diamonds and fur, talks about people behind their backs, goes to get their feet done, but ironically has the balls to bash Black women for having masculine traits. Well, maybe it's because you took all the feminine ones. Yeah, I said it. Hold that for a minute.

We have made our women so insecure that they don't believe in wearing their beautiful natural hair. They bleach their skin. They move away from their Afrocentric beauty because we don't respond positively to it. They want the blonde wigs and blue contacts because we want the blonde wigs and blue contacts. It's bad enough the white mainstream shows bias against our women's beautiful, natural characteristics. We should not contribute to it. With all these chocolate goddesses out here? Y'all boys need help!

We also have the power to force the hand of the entertainment industry. If we stopped supporting music and imagery that hypnotized our children, they would stop inundating us with it. We have the economic power to disrupt that, as well as many other industries. When we weren't treated right on buses they got boycotted and lost money. That's the only reason why things changed. It didn't change because it was the right thing to do. It wasn't because they believed that we should have civil rights. It was money! We don't have to tolerate television and reality shows that embarrass us. We don't have to tolerate people profiting off of caricatures of us that perpetuate the negative stereotypes that we already have trouble shedding. I'm not saying that there is no room for entertainment, but I will say that there needs to be a balance. When I was coming up for every 2 Live Crew, we had five or six A Tribe Called Quests. The balance appears to be in the opposite direction these days. Stop letting the background music and soundtrack to your kid's lives be filled with music that tells them it's cool to engage in unsafe, unhealthy and unintelligent practices. Those celebrities and entertainment executives are not going to be the ones dealing with the fallout that comes from your children following along with it. You will.

Let's talk about some other types of power that we have.

We have the power to increase economic opportunities and growth in our communities. We can open, respect, and patronize our own businesses. We don't have to wait around for other people to do it for us. We certainly would not be successful, or maybe even able to open businesses in other communities.

There is nothing wrong with outsiders coming in, but they do so often without respecting us. They look down at us, treat us poorly, take our money (because we offer it freely), don't provide jobs, and don't circulate money or invest it back with us. It touches every community except ours. It even touches other continents.

We also have the power to stop doing damage to ourselves. Our disadvantages in society do not automatically force us into killing ourselves and each other. For every protest we have about other people inflicting pain upon us, we need to have at least one for when we inflict pain upon our own. I personally consider that to be worse. Even if it seems—or might even be the case—that others don't respect us and our lives, does that mean we don't owe it to ourselves and our people/ families/ children to respect our own lives? We are role modeling how to treat us for the rest of the world to see.

The problem is that we keep giving people reasons to justify the way we are treated. Notice that I did not say "good" reasons, but reasons, nonetheless. As Black men, we can choose not to have these silly beefs with each other. We can stop lying, cheating, robbing, and stealing from each other. We can pool our resources together to make sure everybody eats, as opposed to being cutthroat toward one another. Group economics can solve a lot of the problems we complain about.

People are going to disagree with this, and its fine, but most of the beef that you have with each other is over women. It's nothing more than just the adult version of not liking another boy in class because the girl you like likes him! Some of you will argue that most of the beef is about money. Let's keep it all the way real though. The money is only important because it impacts your relationships with women.

Additionally, while we can refrain from hurting each other, we also have the power to stop abusing women. I'm talking about physically and psychologically. For those of you who do not, God bless you, but don't be fooled into thinking that it does not happen often. Furthermore, you're probably cool with someone who does. Some of you don't know it, but some of you do. Not that you agree with it, but understand that your silence and continued relationship with that man is your acceptance of his actions and behavior. I find it astounding how many perpetrators of domestic violence treat their daughters like gold.

Nobody is even allowed to accidentally bump into their daughters while they continuously and intentionally hurt someone else's daughter. That's not being a man. That's that beta-male bulls#@t that you pull while wanting alpha-male respect. If you are at the point where you feel you need to do that, you are in the wrong relationship.

Some of you even do this, or have done this in front of your children. I mean, it pains me that we even need to talk about this. What kind of man puts his family through that? All the negative things we try to dodge in the world, and some of us bring that into our homes? I can't see how a man, not even a Black man, but a man can want to normalize this for his children. Please seek help. Don't train your son to ruin his life with criminal records. Don't train your daughter to think that finding a man who will put his hands on her is a good thing. We have to be better than that. If you saw it growing up, stop the cycle. If you didn't see it growing up, don't start the cycle. You are right along with us feeling like the criminal justice system does not work in our favor. Why teach your son behaviors to invite the system into his life? You are worried about him getting shot by police, but you are teaching him to be in the position to have police called on him. Talk to a professional.

On the flip side of that. As a Black man you also have the power to remove yourself from relationships where *you* are being abused. Listen, I know what goes on. You don't have to deal with that. We get physically and psychologically abused too. There are better options for you. A lot of times we stay in situations that are not good for us for reasons such as low self-esteem or fear. We may be afraid of our significant others hurting us, threatening us, or leaving us. We may also be afraid to get help due to stigma. Intimate partner violence is underreported, especially when men are the victims. We don't want to be viewed as punks. Check this out. It's easy to just deal with things. It takes strength and courage to address it, demand better, or leave. There are support groups and numbers you can call for help. Think about the kids.

Power is a serious thing, and we have it as Black men. However, we have to look within to see where we can best utilize this power. Just as we can use it to benefit us, we can use it to hurt us. We have to refrain from making things more challenging for ourselves. We have the power to make racists look very stupid out here. The truth is that whenever we are mistreated, harmed, or killed due to racism, the perpetrators justify the actions with victim blaming. I will be clear. Victim blaming is wrong. My intention is not to blame us for our treatment because we all know that a lot of our plight as Black men is a result of residual effects from years of struggle and oppression. However, we could make them look outwardly ridiculous.

If a woman gets sexually harassed at work, it is the action of the perpetrator that is problematic, not the woman's attractiveness or attire. When we get harassed or worse due to explicit or implicit bias, it would be a tremendous help if they were not able to use certain things against us. We give them the feeling of "I told you so" when they do us dirty but are also able to bring up our record of abusing women and children. They feel good when they can defend their actions by pointing out how we were on social media showing off our drug money or items that we obtained during our latest home invasion. They become excited when they can use our attempted murder charges, restraining orders, and petty crime arrest sheets to make the public feel better about what they did to us. I know that many times, we are innocent. This is just to address the times when we are not. We have the power to allow their heinous acts towards us be the focus instead of giving them things they can spin to look like heroes. The only way to make true change is if we work together to do our part in changing the narrative. That's power.

Solidarity is the key word here. These actions will work best if we engage in them in solidarity. The power of numbers, the power of consensus and group action can make personal growth a collective mission for the sake of the community. For the sake of our families. For the sake of our children. Sometimes we men are discouraged from male-related community building because it's seen as exclusive and patriarchal —though patriarchal is not the same as chauvinistic. The bottom line is that male identity is important and needs to be cultivated in a positive way.

STEP THREE TAKEAWAYS

1. We Black men have the ability to change things economically, politically, socially and financially, but we need to work together.

2. You can engage in sexual relationships without fathering a child.

3. Protect our Black women.

ACTIONS TO TAKE

1. Research professionals you can talk to if you need help.

2. Create playlists of positive and clean versions of music that you listen to around your children.

STEP FOUR

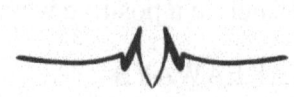

PRESENCE OVER PRESENTS

A whole bunch of gifts and a lot of presents/It's not your presents, it's your presence and the essence/of being there - Edo. G "Be a Father to Your Child"

For the love of God! Stop with the obnoxious spending on top-of-the-line stuff for your kids, man. I'm not saying to be cheap. Do it when necessary. If your child needs a book bag, and you can afford it, definitely get the tough JanSport joint that lasts long as hell. I still have one from many years ago! Don't buy a Gucci book bag, though. We as Black people tend to think that spending more money on something validates us, but what it validates is our fiscal irresponsibility. I'm not knocking anybody's lifestyle or preference for nice things, but let's think about this for a minute.

How many of your friends, relatives, or acquaintances have the newest and latest whatever, but stay asking you for money? Raise your hand.

If you are not raising your hand, then somebody is probably raising their hand thinking about you! I grew up in an all-Black neighborhood on the East Side of Buffalo and went to school at Frederick Law Olmsted Elementary School which was a gifted and talented school in North Buffalo. North Buffalo was the nicest part of the city and was predominantly white. Aside from the racial dynamic, the bottom line is that the neighborhood I went to school in had money, the neighborhood I lived in did not. You probably weren't there but try this anyway:

QUIZ

1. Most of the kids from the _____ had sneakers that cost over $100 per pair.

a). Affluent area

b). Impoverished area

2. The kids that got made fun of for wearing "no name" clothes were from the _____.

a). Affluent area

b). Impoverished area

3. The kids who were left out of the late night erotic movie conversations because they didn't have the advanced cable package at home were from the _____.

a). Affluent area

b). Impoverished area

Answer key: 1-B, 2-A, 3-A

How did you do?! I'm sure you realize the trend. Keep in mind that we are talking about the late 80s and early 90s. Nowadays, that pair of sneakers probably costs between $200 and $300. The must-have clothes in the hood back then were Cross Colors and Karl Kani. They are probably Gucci or Louis Vuitton or something like that now. I don't know. I'm out of the loop. I have been shopping at thrift stores since before it was cool.

Please do not misunderstand me. I am by no means suggesting that the racial wealth gap between Black people and white people in America is because of you buying your child Jordans. What I want is for you to understand a couple of things. First, recognize that you are using your child as an advertisement. Not for any particular product, but as a status symbol for yourself. You are trying to get people to see that you are the baller alpha dad that can afford the obnoxiously expensive clothes. Is your excuse for buying them because he or she looks so adorable in them? Interesting. I wonder if they would not look as adorable to you in nice, new, less expensive items.

Maybe you're competing with a rival dad. The white dads in the suburbs have those passive-aggressive competitions over who grills the best burgers and steaks, or who has the more comfortable man cave for watching football games. The difference is that they have careers, bank accounts, investments, and generational wealth to back their game. We come home to one of the apartments we are renting from them with $1000 outfits texting on $1000 phones without $1000 in the bank. But hey, at least our children are dressed "better" than theirs.

Maybe you're buying the expensive items to prove your love. Listen to me. Don't do that. Stuff gets old, unused, and forgotten. The memories hold the power. Understand and appreciate that power. Your child is more likely to have the fond memories of you taking them out for the day laughing, being silly, taking pictures, and getting ice cream while shopping, than have fond memories of the 30th expensive shirt you bought them. The stuff that is impactful can run a cool $9.00. That shirt that you think is valuable sets you back. I don't care if you have paper or not, it still sets you back. I will explain why shortly.

Is your child even mature enough to realize what they're wearing and how much it costs? I get seriously amused at expensive baby sneakers. I bought a lot of pairs of those trying to overcompensate for my lack of intangibles in my early fatherhood days. I didn't make time, but I bought sneakers. I didn't call regularly, but I bought numerous sets of "My dad is #1" shirts. Pathetic. Who was I trying to convince? Well, I can only speak for myself. Perhaps in your case your baby actually wants expensive sneakers. No? Well in that case, I think the more realistic scenario is that the baby is what I like to call your "ego billboard." An ego billboard is a living, breathing canvas for you to dress up to prove to anyone who will look that your parenting skills are far superior to anybody else's. Congratulations.

See, the problem here is that after all your talk about your children, somehow you still managed to still make things about you. People who understand labels, materialism and prices will recognize how much you spent. But let me ask you a question. How is any of that related to you bonding with your precious baby? You are correct. It is not.

I want you to grasp a couple of concepts. We talked about setting yourself back with expensive purchases. One concept I want to speak with you about is **conspicuous consumption**. This is the idea that people purchase expensive and lavish things to show off their perceived prestige, or sophistication, or affluence. A lot of times we don't have it but pretend like we do. People are always talking about "fake it till you make it."

What people leave out is the fact that most people don't make it precisely because they fake it. That energy should be going to something substantial to benefit your little ones. To quote Ghostface Killah from the almighty Wu-Tang Clan, "Don't front for me man! If you gonna play that role man, play it though!" You're buying things so that people can see that you can afford it even if you can't afford it. Your clothes are more expensive than those of Mark Zuckerberg, Jeff Bezos, Bill Gates, and Warren Buffett. *That my friend, is a problem.*

The second concept I want to familiarize you with is **opportunity cost**. People tend to only factor in the actual price tag of something. For example, you might say "Damn, these jeans only cost $150! They are usually around $300!" Exciting, right? That's because in your mind you "saved" $150. On the flip side, here is what people who understand opportunity cost might say, "Man, those jeans are nice, but my daughter is 5-years old. If I *don't* buy the jeans, and invest the $150 in an investment account, I could put in like $150 a month until she's 18, and on her 18th birthday, I could give her about $25,000." You think I'm bugging, right?

Do this exercise with me. Pull up a compound interest calculator on your phone, computer, tablet, or whatever. Got it? Perfect. Now, for the initial balance, put in $150 (the jeans). For contribution, put in either $150 monthly, or $1800 annually (your coffee, fast food, and weed money). For interest rate, input a modest 6% or so. For years to grow, put in 13 (18th birthday of a 5-year-old). Compound one time annually. Hit enter. What did you get? That's your opportunity cost, my brother. Those jeans didn't save you $150, they cost you that amount on your screen on your daughter's 18th birthday. That could be her down payment on her first home. I know that's young, but she could even go off to college and rent her house out to earn income so she can focus on her studies and not be strapped for cash. You could literally give her a house for her birthday. She could be a property owner at 18 years old because of your decision making and patience. She could also live there and rent out rooms while she attends a local college to both earn money and save on expenses. She could use it to start her business. She could use it to invest in other things she is interested in. She could travel the world and visit places you only dreamed about visiting.

She could save it until she is older and more mature. You could break her off a piece of it and tell her that her birthday gift is $10,000 and secretly save the rest for her when she turns 21. You could provide her with a financial vehicle to make her independent, so she won't be impressed by some no-good boy with a little bit of money in his pocket. Most importantly, you can teach her how you did it. She can teach your grandchildren how to do it. Then it goes on and on until your bloodline experiences that mighty generational wealth that you always hear about. The choice is yours, Black man. Close your eyes and imagine that. How does it feel? Is it better than trendy clothes or whatever else you are doing to live above your means? Even if you are not living above your means, it's still an opportunity to come up. Play around with some numbers and see what kind of things you can do for your children besides using them to make yourself look good and teaching them to be materialistic.

A close friend of mine who is basically my brother decided to send his teenage son out of town for a while because he was hanging with the wrong crowd and getting negatively influenced. This is going to be funny because I didn't tell him that I was going to put this in here! Anyway, he scraped up money for a plane ticket and assistance to the selected out-of-town relative who was going to help out. Now, many of us are living paycheck to paycheck, so abrupt expenses of that magnitude can put you on your back for a minute. I was popped too, so I couldn't really help much. After the ticket was secured, and the arrangements were made I felt relieved, but my friend was still stressing. I'm like, "What's the problem?" He said that he could not afford the luggage. I said, "Nonsense!" I looked on Craigslist and in about 8 seconds I found a full set of nice new-looking Samsonite luggage for sale for $30. I mean, it was a full 4-piece set. It was a clean, navy blue set with a large, medium, small, and a little carry on for a mere $30! I showed my friend, and he said, "I can't send him out of town with used luggage." I had to hang it up after that. Keep in mind, this dude is literally one of the best fathers I know.

I clearly forgot that ever since we were kids, he always wanted top-of-the-line everything. His parents would give him and his sister the same amount of money for Christmas shopping. His sister would come back with a whole new wardrobe and gifts for everybody. He would come back with a shirt and two pairs of jeans. That day with the luggage I realized that his attitude about appearances persisted even as an adult in a time crunch for a last-minute flight to get his teenage son to safety. If my son would have been in trouble, I would have sent his ass out on the first thing smoking with a contractor bag from Home Depot if I had to. That's real. Some things just don't matter.

We have to understand depreciation. That is the decrease in value of something over time. When you buy new, you pay a lot because of the middleman. If you get it second-hand, once you've used it a bit, it's as used as it would be if you bought it already used, you know! Why shoulder the cost of the depreciation? Let someone else do it and pocket the difference.

It's like the huge difference between the price of a brand-new car vs. the price of a really nice used car. In this case, the suitcases might have been used once. Or never, and were part of some old person's estate who passed away before they could use them...once your kid takes the luggage with them on the trip (and used luggage is PERFECT for a kid), no one knows the difference. Also, nobody cares.

STEP FOUR TAKEAWAYS

1. Your time and attention are what your kids need, not the things you buy.
2. You can make better financial decisions.
3. Opportunity costs are things that you miss out on when you spend a certain way.

ACTIONS TO TAKE

1. Take a financial literacy course, talk to someone who understands money, or read financial literacy books.
2. Teach your children strategies (savings, investing, giving).
3. Create a budget for yourself, allocate money to certain things and stick to it.

STEP FIVE

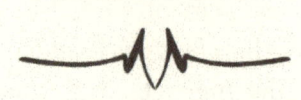

EMBRACE PULCHRITUDE

I'm a part spiritual/Part paraphysical miracle/And I'mma black out in a minute too

- Canibus "Let's Ride"

When I was in 7th grade, my math teacher, Mr. Montante, and I had a pretty good relationship. He was one of the many teachers who knew I had a bad home situation, but was one of only a few teachers who cared. I never forgot about that. While I'm at it, let me take a minute to also thank Mrs. Appleby for planting the seed of my love and appreciation for classical music. Thank you to Mrs. Gascon for teaching me French and allowing me to have pizza on pizza days because she knew I couldn't afford the 50 cents. Also, thank you to Ms. Diffine for teaching me how to write (all those damn overhead projector notes!), and most importantly, helping me write a letter to Hutch-Tech High School after I was rejected to explain that the only reason why I missed a lot of school was due to problems at home. They never responded by the way.

So, back to the story! I had a huge crush on this girl named "Elle" and I always talked about her. I would always tell Mr. Montante about how pretty, smart, and quiet she was. Even as a young boy, I never liked those attention-seeking, loud-for-no-reason type of girls! Even though "Elle" liked me for me, my problem was that I didn't have confidence because I was poor, had problems at home, had worn-out clothes, always needed a haircut, and most importantly, because I wasn't that smart. I mean, maybe I was, but because I was rarely in school, my grades were terrible. It's not that I would ditch school or didn't want to learn though. Remember when I told you that my father was in a bad place due to his addiction? Well, I missed a lot of school because he actually threatened my mother and told her that he was going to shoot me and my brother in the morning at the bus stop. She finally had the courage to take us and leave after years of torment. She notified the school of the threat, and we got put on home instruction. They basically just mailed work to the house. So even though it was accounted for, I had terrible attendance on record. I'm still tight about that because I couldn't get into any of the good high schools I wanted to go to. Plus, I wanted to follow "Elle!"

Anyway, Mr. Montante told me to impress my crush with some sophisticated vocabulary. I had not too long before learned about this play about this dude named Cyrano de Bergerac. Cyrano was crazy nice with the words. He was a poet. He was also a great artist and musician. The thing was, he had a real big nose and lacked confidence just like I did. Cyrano was in love with this girl named Roxane but knew he wouldn't have a shot because he was not attractive. Matter of fact, I think she was his cousin! Anyway, Roxane was into a guy named Christian who was handsome, but had no game. Cyrano then wrote fly letters and poems to Roxane pretending to be Christian. There was the famous scene where Christian was on the ground talking to Roxane who was in her window. Cyrano was in the bushes feeding him lines to say to her. Roxane fell in love with the poet. I wanted to be the poet. Mr. Montante told me to tell "Elle" that she was pulchritudinous! I couldn't even say it at first. He had me look it up and sure enough, it meant beautiful. It was the perfect word to describe her.

Okay, so I punked out and never told "Elle" and actually told Ms. Diffine instead! But listen up anyway! When I say embrace pulchritude, I'm going way deeper than vanity. I'm talking about your overall attractiveness. I know you look suave with your wavy hair, your nice locs, your freshly tightened braids, your curly afro, or your sexy bald head.

I know you feel nice with the fresh shave, trim up, or brushed beard. I'll admit, you clean up nice, but when I speak about attraction, I mean by law.

There's no point in you getting all done up when you're not right inside. The universe knows it. Yes, we are talking about laws of attraction. The cute girl at the checkout in the mall might be fooled by your vanity with little substance, but the universe is not. In being attractive, you need to attract more than superficial attention. You have the power to attract positive energy, happiness, love, relationships, peace, wealth, and anything else that you claim you want and need. Let's have a crash course about beauty and attractiveness.

I want to describe a typical morning for me. I wake up early. I like to get up in the morning because I feel like the world is all mine. While many people are sleeping in, there is less noise and commotion. I get to appreciate the sounds of the birds and the light breeze. I open up the doors and the windows to let the fresh air and morning energy in. I then light my diffuser with lemongrass oil for aromatherapy. I hook up the Bluetooth speaker and put on calm, relaxing meditation music. I get some nice stretching in and just sit and relax. I take this time to practice mindfulness and just be present with myself. I'm not worrying about troubles, deadlines, or any other stressors. I meditate.

When I say meditate, I don't mean that I am sitting in the middle of the floor with my legs crossed chanting! I mean, that's cool too, but that is not what I do. I take in the sounds, the smells, the energy, the appreciation for life and I go somewhere.

Where I go while I'm meditating depends on the day. Sometimes I go on vacation to the Caribbean and listen to the ocean waves roll up on the beach from my balcony suite. Sometimes I go back to a pleasant time or fun event that I had in my life. Sometimes I go to places I have never been and concentrate on them because I know that I will be there someday soon. Somewhere like a small bakery in Italy, or buying something from a little shop in a small, quaint town in Germany. Sometimes I sit on the beach off the coast of West Africa. I do these visits on a spiritual level because I understand something very powerful that I want you to understand also.

Your brain does not recognize that you are not physically in a place. So, as far as your brain knows, you were actually there. This is why you can imagine something and change your mood. Listen, how do you feel when you think about that dude that stole from you? How do you feel when you think about a traumatic time that you went through? You feel upset. You feel scared, and it's real, like, you can feel it. That is because as far as your brain goes you just lived through it again. That's why your heart beats fast and you get worked up and start sweating. So, if that is the case, couldn't you do the opposite and psych yourself out in a positive way? The answer is an emphatic YES! That is why I do it, and why you should do it too. Take your trip with your kids. Let your mind and your body live it. Listen to them laughing, and see them running. It doesn't have to be anywhere extravagant. It could be your backyard, or the neighborhood playground. Simple.

Now, after I take my trip, or relive an incredible experience I had, I get ready to experience my amazing day. This is because I already know that my day is going to be amazing. I pick up my journal, and I write out my day. You see, I don't go running out of my house on a daily basis and just let whatever happens happen. No, sir! I plan out my day. I write out what I am going to do, how great it's going to be and the most important part, who I am going to help. I cannot stress that enough. You need to help people. Make time to help people. Remember, we are being attractive to the universe. So even if you feel like you need help, help someone else. This is the type of positive energy that you need cycling back to you, especially at this point in time. If you want good things, you need to give good things.

The beauty in that is that some days I can literally write, "I am going to visit somebody who may be going through something" or "I am going to help my child with a science project" or "I am going to get rid of all those bottles I saved in my trunk and give them to the guy that walks around and collects cans in the neighborhood." It can be anything big or small. You can also just say, "I am going to do good for somebody today" without an actual plan. That will put you in the helping mindset and you will be surprised at how it impacts you and your day.

I remember one time I saw a group of kids playing basketball without a basketball. They were using one of those thin rubber balls from a supermarket or something. The real light ones that just blow away in the wind. I had a bunch of old basketballs in my car from when I used to play (before them knees got bad!). I pulled over, got out, and opened the trunk. I grabbed the balls and said, "Yo!" and got their attention. There were three of them. I had four balls in the car. I threw long passes to them from the street to the court. They went nuts! They thanked me repeatedly and had the biggest smiles on their faces. I said to them, "You don't have to thank me, just practice hard." I then drove off and had them on my mind all day. I thought about the privilege of being able to bring three young Black boys joy from one small act. All I did was give them something that I didn't even need. I rode that feeling all day. I didn't plan it. I just *saw* the opportunity because I was *looking* for an opportunity to help someone from writing it out that morning. So, after I write out my day, I jump on my bike and hit the bike trail (weather permitting). Again, it's early and peaceful. Only a few like-minded people are out there. It is usually older people walking to stay active, or that heavy set person power walking with that inspiring determination to lose weight. We see each other every morning and have a mutual respect for our similarities of being out there daily on our grind. This is all positive energy I am picking up along with the physical workout. I am riding and listening to something inspirational or educational. I have an audiobook going, or a motivational speech while I am getting a sweat. Please understand that I'm not listening to songs about killing other Black men, selling drugs to other Black people, or mistreating Black women. There may be a time and place for that kind of vibe, but this is not it. I know I might have hit a nerve with some of y'all with that, but I'm confident you will get over it.

    If you want to test out my logic, think about sitting with your son or daughter while listening to one of those songs. Now think about sitting with your son or daughter while listening to "Lovely Day" by Bill Withers. If you don't see the difference in energy holler at me, so I can write you a different book! Anyway, I do the bike trail from beginning to end and experience the greenery and watch the squirrels, chipmunks, and sometimes deer. I then head home pumped up because most people aren't even up yet and I already meditated, stretched, journaled, enjoyed nature, had positive human interaction, and worked out.

So, I am feeling accomplished BEFORE I actually leave the house to start my day. Indescribable.

I get home, put the bike away, go shower, get dressed, and eat some fruit and drink some water, or make a protein shake. I sit down to enjoy it while feeling refreshed, go say goodbye to the love of my life and those beautiful children and head out to handle some business. What is also good is that I get to work early, and people start dragging in looking like they hate life. They are moping, have poor body language, are complaining already and are using Tim Horton's coffee to try to wake up and get going for the day. Meanwhile, I'm feeling like I'm ready to go cliff diving or something! I would like to stress that ALL of this is the result of choice. None of these things just happens to me. I make the choice every day, and part of my good feeling is not only the results, but the fact that I am determining my own time and outcomes. That's how you approach that. It's invigorating.

Now, I understand that based on some people's schedule that might not be feasible, but some of you just don't get up because you're doing a bunch of nothing all night. Stop that. You have goals. You are reading this book so it's clear you have goals. Is the time you are spending bringing you closer to those goals? If not, change how you are spending or better yet wasting your time. You can't expect things to change in your life if you don't make life changes. Did you hear that? Read that again. If you don't waste time and just have a different schedule, its fine. Do what works for you at whatever time. Either way, get your journal on to plan your day. Also, meditate and take those trips with those babies!

STEP FIVE TAKEAWAYS
1. You can create your own reality by taking an active role in planning your days.
2. The positive energy that you put out circles back to you.
3. Your small everyday choices shape your achievements and outcomes.

ACTIONS TO TAKE
1. Buy a nice journal and a nice pen.
2. Every morning, take a few minutes to write about what you appreciate, what you are going to do for the day, and who you are going to help.
3. Schedule some exercise in your daily routine.

STEP SIX

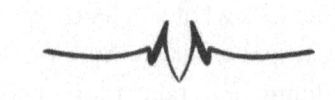

STOP ADVERTISING YOUR PROBLEMS

You never have the story, right and exact/and then you always try to bore me with your yakkity yak - Run DMC "You Talk Too Much"

Hear me loud and clear. You need to understand and accept the fact that nobody cares. Ouch, right?! When I tell you to understand that nobody cares, I don't mean that nobody cares about *you*. What I mean is that nobody cares about your excuses, your lackluster reasoning, your so-called logic, your empty promises, your self-praise, or your self-deprecating rhetoric. If you feel like you are not being appreciated as a father, then step your game up. Who wants to hear a grown man pat himself on the back for performing the expected duties of fatherhood? I remember on the comedy special "Bring the Pain," Chris Rock was mocking you saying, "I take care of my kids." You know his response? "You're supposed to you dumb m%*$#@!

You're sitting around talking about how you're the best father to ever grace the Earth. Check this out. You meet a nice young lady and get to know her a little bit. She is really beautiful, smart, sophisticated, funny, and accomplished. She is the total package. The two of you hit it off and arrange a coffee date and meet up on a different occasion. You're very excited! You tell your friends about the potential mate that just came into your life. You haven't felt this way in quite some time. You talk to your relatives about her. You think about her non-stop in anticipation for the big first date. Then the day and time comes. Yes, lawd!

You get there, and she is looking even finer than she was when you met her. You have your quick reunion and get to the date. Then, the whole time you're out on the patio at the coffee spot she rambles on and on, "I am such a beautiful woman," "I am so much smarter than other girls," "I am really sophisticated," "Can't you see how funny I am?" and to top it off, " Wow, I am really accomplished." Over and over during the date she says these things. Even though they are accurate statements, would you want to date her again? Probably not. The reason why is because it's different when you said she was beautiful, smart, funny, and accomplished. When she assigned those attributes to herself it came off as pompous, annoying, and flat-out obnoxious.

The woman who has those attributes and is confident enough to refrain from announcing it, is a boss. That's what you need to understand. If you know you're a good father, be one. Who are you trying to convince by reminding everybody who will listen about the stuff you bought, or meals you prepared or the time you kept your own damn kids for a period of time? You can't be serious. Are you bragging about doing homework or attending the piano recitals of your own children? I hope not, and if you are, shame on you. You're better than that. You can get better or bitter, but you cannot have both.

I would like to walk you through a powerful lesson that I learned as a child. When I was about 8-years old, we were having a family party. You know, one of those old school ghetto family functions where you see the cousins that you don't see regularly, and you all act shy and then warm up to each other and start having mad fun late as hell right before it's time to go and then you don't want to leave? Yeah, one of those! All the adults were in the kitchen smoking that reefer. Yes, I dated myself and said reefer! Remember my time frames. This is the mid-80s. There was no kush and blunts. It was reefer and Tops rolling papers.

I had just got an Optimus Prime transformer toy and it was my pride and joy. I didn't get a lot of toys and that was the best toy in the game at that time. It was so expensive that my mother didn't let me take it to the party, but I wanted to show it off. I was pissed. I never had the chance to be the envy at the party, and now I was being held back by my own mother! What a hater. Since I didn't have it with me, I told everybody who would listen about it. That toy was something serious. Optimus Prime was a truck and the trailer opened up and a separate car named "Roller" would come out and down the ramp by itself. Some of the O.G.s reading this book are smiling right now!

My Aunt Donna came out of the adults'-section to check on us kids. I was like, "Hey Aunt Donna! I got the new Optimus Prime!" She looked me right in my face and said, "No, you don't." I said, "Yes I do!! It has a car named Roller that comes out when you open the trailer!" Aunt Donna came back, "No you don't." I was so mad I got loud, "YES I DO! IT IS AT HOME! MY MOM WOULDN'T LET ME BRING IT!" Aunt Donna, straight face, "No, you don't." I wanted to scream! I was thinking to myself, "What is wrong with her?" In my fit of rage, I did the unthinkable and ran into the adult's only reefer section to find my mother. "Ma! Would you PLEASE tell Aunt Donna that I got the new Optimus Prime at home?"

My mother said, "Boy, if you don't get the f%$ out of this f&%$ kitchen, I will f&*^ you the f&%$ up!"

In Step Three we talked about our women being rough due to how we treat them. This is a clear example of that. My mother used to be one of the sweetest, kindest, most feminine women in the world. After years of dealing with her own father and mine, she turned straight vicious.

After the verbal lashing, I ran out of that kitchen as fast as I could to only to find Aunt Donna cracking up like nobody's business! I'm crying out of fear of getting in trouble when I get home, embarrassment for getting sonned (pun intended) in front of everybody, and frustration that I couldn't convince Aunt Donna that I had the new Optimus Prime.

"Why are you laughing?" I asked (cried).

Aunt Donna said to me, "Do you have the new Optimus Prime?"

"Yes," I said.

Aunt Donna then changed my life with this one. Her response, "Then what difference does it make that somebody doesn't believe you?" Smack. She continued, "As long as you know the truth, that's all that matters. Don't waste your time trying to impress people." Smack again.

She knew. She knew it would bother me that I couldn't convince her. She knew I would run into the kitchen to get someone to corroborate my story. Most importantly, she knew how her sister, my mother would respond to me for asking for verification of a toy purchase at a grown folk's party. She played me like a fiddle in order to teach me a valuable lesson. I held on to that my whole life. I'm not even sure if she remembers that. Hopefully, she will read this and know how much I appreciate it.

The moral of the story is that you don't need to go around announcing that you are a good father. Just be a good father. It should be like breathing. It's built in and you just do it. You don't walk around letting everybody know that you are a great breath taker. Why? Because you're better than that. Back in the day, we used to say, "Don't talk about it, walk about it" or "Don't talk about it, be about it." Either way, be such a good father that everybody says it for you. And if they don't, be okay with it. You know the truth. Even more, your children will, and they will not be able stop saying so.

The kids won't be able to stop talking about you and how you're the best. It will be deep love and pride, not competitive and about who got the most stuff. It won't be ego-driven, but love-driven, which has a radically different feeling. People can tell if the story the kid is telling is about ego or deep admiration and respect. They will talk about you with that love and admiration long after you are gone from this earth, and your grandchildren will tell the stories that they heard from their parents, and everyone will try to follow your example. That how you leave a legacy!

STEP SIX TAKEAWAYS

1. You don't have time for excuses, you need to take action.

2. You also don't have time to blow your own horn all day, you need to take action.

3. Let your beautiful relationship with your children speak for itself.

ACTIONS TO TAKE

1. Write down or type up all your positive attributes. Ask others you trust what they believe are your best traits.

2. Keep them in a place where you see them regularly.

3. Write down or type up a checklist of things that you would like to improve in your life and how you will work to achieve them.

4. Keep that list with you and aggressively work to check items off to feel the progress.

STEP SEVEN

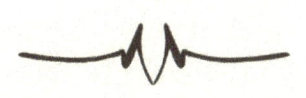

KEEP YOUR PROMISES

Ask me if his daddy was sick of us/Cause you ain't never pick him up

- Lupe Fiasco "He Say She Say"

Out of all the most difficult things in my life growing up, the disappointment was the worst. I took extension cord beatings, didn't have much food, periods of no gas or electric, roaches, rats, and the whole nine. That stuff I got used to. What I could never get used to was the pain of waiting to be picked up only to have it not happen. On the real, that scarred me so bad that I refuse to wait for people even now. This is a true story; when my wife and I were younger, I instituted a rule. If we were supposed to go somewhere, she was not allowed to use the words "I'm ready" unless she was sitting in the car. I'm dead serious! All that saying she's ready but still taking time in mirror with hair and trying on 37 outfits was not working for me.

That is not specific to my wife. That is for anybody.

The other side of that is that I make it worse on myself because of my trauma. If I tell somebody I am on the way, I am *actually* on the way. How many times have you told somebody that you were on the way while you were still in the house? That's foul. So, because I'm always early, and the other person is often late, the waiting period is often extended for me, which makes me irate.

That is how the let downs with my father used to go. He would tell me with all good intentions that he was going to take me to the "Wreck." This was the old basketball court in my neighborhood on Delavan and Moselle on the East Side of Buffalo. In my later years I realized that it was actually the "Rec" as in recreation center! I wanted to learn how to play basketball.

"Dad, can you take me to the Wreck?" I would ask. He would say, "Yeah, let me take care of a few things and we can go when I get back." I would be ecstatic. Due to my excitement, I would get ready early. I would turn down invites from other kids in the neighborhood to play football. I would refuse trips to walk to the store, or do anything. I would not run the risk of missing him when he got back.

...And I would wait.

I would rationalize and say things like, "Well, if he comes now, we still have a little while before it gets dark." Then it would get dark. Then I would say, "Well, maybe the streetlights will provide enough light to see the rim." Then I would get sleepy. Then my mother would say, "Junior, your father is not coming." Then I would get upset and say, "Yes, he is. You just don't want me to have fun." Then he wouldn't come. Just like last time. Just like the time before last time. Since it would happen over and over, each time would make me say to myself, "Well, something came up the last five times, so this one *has* to the be the time. A lot of you may know this feeling. A lot may not. Doesn't matter. Don't do this to your children. It's mental torture. In fact, it's more than mental. Its profound emotional torture, grief, and fear. If you cannot do something, tell them. If you don't feel like doing something, tell them. If there is a chance something will prevent you from doing something, tell them. If you make plans with them, clear your schedule. DO NOT overbook yourself and bump your kid's time. DO NOT make promises that you can't keep. Things beyond your control can take place. I don't care if you promise to bring a piece of candy back when you get home. Don't even say it unless it is already in your possession as you are driving home.

You know kids don't forget! They will tell you without hesitation, "You said last Thursday that you would take me to get a green lollipop today before you took off your shoes to relax after work." Also, your kids are probably hella smart, so they might have snuck up on you and got you to agree while you were half asleep! You have to watch out for that!

On a serious note though, think about the consequences of flat out breaking your promises to your children. Imagine teaching your daughter that she should get used to empty promises. Think about her stumbling into an abusive relationship and keep falling for the line, "Oh, baby, I promise I will change." What she will understand is, "Hey, I love my dad. It used to take him seven or eight times before he would actually come through with what he promised. I love this guy too. This has already been the fifth time he's punched me in the face. All I have to do is just hang in there a little while longer and things will finally be good for me." Wow.

Imagine teaching your son that he should get used to empty promises. Think about him deciding to run with a gang and falling for the line, "We are your only family, we will always be there for you." What he will understand is, "I know these dudes got me doing dirt, but they have always come through for me every time I needed them. They told me that they would bail me out and get me a lawyer if I get caught. They have always come through for me unlike my father." Wow.

Listen, our kids are let down enough out here. We don't need to contribute to that. And I don't want to hear that "they need to understand that things don't always go as planned." Yeah, I agree, **but let them learn that from people outside of their support system.** You can tell them that. You don't need to be the one who lets them down. They need to know that their father has their back when **NO ONE** else does. They should be able to experience disappointment from elsewhere, but always know that their father stays true to his word and always comes correct. Remember how fragile those little ones are. It's a big deal, my brother. Do you remember that episode of "The Fresh Prince of Bel-Air" when Will's father came back around? When you are done with this book, go back and watch the end scene between Will and Uncle Phil. Those who know, know. Keep your promises, man.

STEP SEVEN TAKEAWAYS

1. Breaking promises to children devastates them even when you don't think it is a big deal.

2. You may be teaching them not to count on you.

3. Keeping your word is an expression of your care and concern for a person, especially a child.

ACTIONS TO TAKE

1. Don't speak in absolutes when making plans. Things come up. Leave space for that.

2. Create weekly schedules and practice sticking with them. It will settle you're routine.

3. Let your reliability speak for itself as you show up consistently over time. (If trust is already broken, it will take time to build back up.).

STEP EIGHT

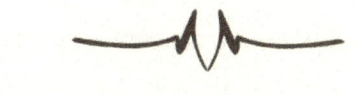

PRACTICE SELF-CARE

Cause' true wealth comes from good health and wise ways/we gotta start taking better care of ourselves - Dead Prez "Be Healthy"

The social worker in me wouldn't let me complete this guide without mentioning self-care. All through those years I was training to be a social worker and social justice advocate, the common theme was self-care. So, here is the beauty of self-care. It is subjective. Some people go for quiet walks to reflect. Some join a recreational sports league. Some read, some write. You can get a massage, take a bike ride, or take in a movie. You can rest. You can go to church, you can practice an instrument, you can learn a language, you can go to the gym, you can turn off your phone, you can see a counselor.

Self-care is basically any activity that we do that takes care of our mental, emotional, and physical health. Engaging in regular self-care is an excellent way to reduce stress, anxiety, and fatigue. Some benefits include things like lowering heart rate and other physiological processes that lead to premature aging and chronic conditions. This is important for us Black men because we are already susceptible to a lot of stress-induced physiological arousal that puts us at risk. A lot of this is the result of living the everyday stresses we face as Black men in society.

Self-care is also key to more positive relationships, especially with our children. As a person and as a father, you need to take care of your mental health. We spend so much time ripping and running that we forget to look out for ourselves. We need tune ups, and as Black people, we have been very reluctant to take advantage of counseling services. We think it makes us weak. We don't trust people. We men don't like to share our inner thoughts. We don't have time for that. We don't have the money. Our insurance doesn't cover it. There are no Black therapists. That's white people stuff. It doesn't work. We don't want anybody in our business. We have done just fine without it.

Remember, this is about the kids. What we are doing by assigning a negative connotation to counseling is eliminating a resource that can help us with our children. I say something like that shouldn't be written off. I will also add that counseling does not always look like it does on television with you laying on that brown leather couch and the condescending person in a suit is taking notes and judging you, or not taking notes and doodling and just taking your money. Many counselors look just like you. I look just like you. You also don't have to commit to going to a counselor every week for the rest of your life. You can go and speak to somebody once, twice, or just a few times.

Check and see if your job has an EAP (Employee Assistance Program). These are typically services paid for by your employer and offered through an outside agency that provides confidential counseling services. So, in other words, if you work for the company, and you're feeling depressed, stressed, going through something, battling addiction, family problems (hint, hint), or anything else, you can contact the EAP and set up sessions. They are free to you and your job won't even know. The job pays for it, but has no connection with who utilizes it. Check with your human resources department.

Another thing related to self-care is nutrition. Pay attention to your diet, bro. I'm going to keep it real with you. Your daily numerous cups of coffee, sugar soda throughout the day, fast food on the run, and drinking-as-soon-as-you-get-home-lifestyle is tearing you apart from your kids. Sounds crazy, but listen. When you got your new car, you pulled up to the gas station flossing, whipped out your credit card and paid at the pump for the top of the line premium unleaded fuel. While the gas was pumping you took the squeegee and cleaned your windows, took out your mats and shook them out. You pulled out that gum wrapper that was stuck in between the seat and the arm rest. You did that because you want only the best for your new car.

The odd thing is that your body has been riding with you from day one, and you don't put nearly as much effort into it. How do you take care of it? Your car gets the highest-octane fuel, and your body gets the junk. Then you have the audacity to complain about how tired you are. You feel drained. You're edgy and agitated. Your kids get on your nerves when you get home, or you cancel going to visit them because you're worn out. News flash, my man. You're not drained because that would suggest that you had something substantial in your system to lose in the first place. You were never properly fueled up. You are not nourishing yourself properly because you don't understand the correlation between your diet and your mood. You don't understand the link between getting sufficient rest and your mood. You don't understand the impact of drugs and alcohol on your mood. If you cannot function, you are of no use to your children. If you cannot function, you are actively working against your plan of repairing or strengthening the relationship. Nothing is more comical to me than 19-year old students who come to my 8:00 am classes, eating a bag of M & M's and sipping on a bottle of Mountain Dew complaining about life and dragging around like they are 85-years old.

Take time to eat better. Lay off the things that slow you down. Remember that you are a role model. You are a superhero to your kids. If you aren't yet, you will be. You are the biggest, strongest guy they know. Don't teach them that you have to eat like garbage, refrain from sleep and mistreat their bodies to get that way.

STEP EIGHT TAKEAWAYS

1. You must take time to take care of yourself, and you should not feel guilty about it.

2. There doesn't need to be a negative connotation to counseling services.

ACTIONS TO TAKE

1. Schedule a self-care activity at least once a week (sports, walks, movie, church, or whatever you see fit).

2. Do some healthy meal planning for yourself and your children.

3. Look into your employment benefits and see what services are available (i.e., EAP).

4. Seek help for addiction/mental health services if necessary.

STEP NINE

LET GO OF THE PAST

Promise to never leave him even if his mama tweakin'/Cause my dad left me and I promised to never repeat him - Jay-Z "New Day"

Remember in Step Five when we talked about going on vacation? Your mind can't tell the difference between you imagining laying on the beach feeling the sun and hearing the waves crashing from you actually laying on the beach feeling the sun and hearing the waves crashing. That's powerful stuff. That is exactly why you have to let go of the past my brother. I know things were hard for you. I know you tried and failed many times over. Take the growth opportunity from it as opposed to dwelling on it. That causes stagnation. That does not help you tighten things up with the little ones. We are working on *pro*gression, not *re*gression.

Accept that you messed up. Everyone great has messed up somewhere on their path to greatness. You cannot take it back. What's done is done.

What you *can* do is stop the impact of your mistakes from lingering on forever. Don't beat yourself up anymore. You have done enough of that. Society has done enough of that. Forgive yourself. For a long time, I didn't forgive myself and it caused me to continue to make mistakes because my head was not in the right place. I don't want that happening to you, or continuing to happen to you. You have suffered enough. We have to show that resilience. You have to face that past. Defeat those inner demons so that you can level up. No, it is not easy and yes, you are afraid.

   You stay away because your kids are living, breathing reminders of mistakes that you have made. The kids themselves are not the mistakes, but some of the circumstances around them are riddled with errors. That's hard to deal with. That is your insecurity causing you to hate their mother, their maternal uncles, aunts, cousins, and grandparents. But if you are being honest, you know that they are not supposed to side with you. Is your kids' maternal grandmother supposed to appreciate your absence and lack of effort? Is their maternal grandfather supposed to respect the hands-off approach you take with his grandchildren? You wouldn't. Don't try to change the rules when it comes to you. It doesn't work like that. In fact, think about it like this: they and you are actually on the same page: everyone is trying to protect the children. Let your reliability speak for itself.

Speaking of mistakes, you may need to accept that *she* messed up. I'm sorry to hear that, but how long has it been now? Wow, that's a lot of power she has over you. She did you wrong then and you can't move on now. You're wasting valuable time. Some relationships just aren't meant to be, and you know that. You need to be okay with that.

I will use myself as an example. My wife is hands-down the best thing that has ever happened to me. I cringe when I think about how there was a time in my life when I wanted nothing more than to work things out with my eldest daughter's mother who was absolutely no good for me. I would have given anything to be with her so that we could remain a family. God is good. Sometimes you don't understand just how good until later on. We spoke about opportunity cost in the presence-over-presents step, and how buying some things means that you can't buy others. When I think about how the opportunity cost for forcing that relationship would have been my beautiful wife, it sends me into a near panic attack. That's real. I had nightmares about it for years.

The relationships that are meant to be are between you and your kids. You should not let your lack of ability to let go of the past cause your son or daughter to ask their mom why you don't love them. That's cruelty if I ever heard it, my brother.

It's cruel that you are alive and well and didn't make it to the graduation. It's terrible that he took off his helmet after he scored that touchdown and didn't see you even though you said you would be there. It's unthinkable that she got a standing ovation for her solo in the school musical and you missed it because you're stuck in the past.

Stop letting fear hold you back. Here is the thing. The situation is way worse in your head. You spend all this time worrying about it and replaying the worst-case scenario in your mind. You're like, "If I come around, they're going to…," or "Man, their mother is always…" What you will come to realize is when you take that first step to re-establish yourself, you'll be like "Oh, that wasn't as bad as I thought it would be." It's like when you had anxiety about going to school when you were younger. You would be dreading it from the night before, and extra tired and upset in the morning. But once you got to school, you saw your friends and the teacher might have been absent and you had a substitute! It turned out to be a pretty good day. It was way worse in your head back then, and that still stands now.

Know that this fear is not just on you. Many of us have been trained to be afraid. You are a product of your environment. What I mean is, as a Black man, you have had to worry about how people perceive you.

You have had to worry about interactions with the police. You had to change the way you talk, walk and dress out of fear of not being accepted and getting a spot. We have Black artists in hip hop and pop culture who are afraid to use their power and influence to help our people out of fear of losing money and fame. Instead, we get messages to our children that glorify irresponsible sexual behavior, drug distribution and use, terrible money advice, and unnecessary violence towards people who look like them. We listen to it, watch it, and allow our kids to do the same out of fear of not being "cool."

We are trained to be afraid to try. Afraid to fail. Afraid to leave the hood so people won't call us a sellout. Afraid to be open to conservative viewpoints so we won't be called an *"Uncle Tom"* or a *"House Nigger"* (both of which are used in the wrong context). Afraid to look broke and be rich instead of look rich and be broke. We are scared to show love out of fear of looking weak. Scared to be ourselves. Scared to speak up. Scared to think for ourselves. Scared to be vulnerable. Scared of being exposed for acting tough, but actually feeling scared.

If you haven't been involved, your kids will still welcome you. Based on where they are developmentally, you may have challenges, but reintegration is tricky, especially for kids. You may have to work hard, but so be it. You might get push back, and I say that's a good thing. Your children shouldn't be taught to allow people to freely walk in and out of their lives without consequence. You have to earn back the trust. You may not feel like you are making progress, but don't let that be a deterrent. How many times have you pretended to hate something that you actually loved? That's what the kids may do, but you gotta eat that. You have to meet them where they are and give them what they need. Remember, this is not about you, it's about them.

You are afraid of what everybody thinks except for the ones you should be worried about. The children. You are afraid that you don't measure up. You're afraid of coming up short. You're afraid of being hurt. You are a Black man. Handle your business. Stop with the short-term thinking. We have to play the long game.

It may be one of the hardest things you ever do in your life, but you have to keep pushing. Keep showing up. Keep taking blows of rejection. I mean take it over and over and keep coming. Prove that you can't stop because they mean too much to you. Take notes. Document the days, times, and outcomes. Keep a calendar. Write that on Tuesday, March 17th at 6:49 pm, you called your son and he refused to come to the phone. Note that his mother did not seem to help him come around. Note that you told her to tell him that you love him and will try again tomorrow.

On Wednesday, March 18th, at 6:31 pm write that you called, and nobody answered the phone even though you know they were home. Leave a message that you love him and you will try again tomorrow. Document that as well. You may cry, yell, and scream out of frustration, but do all that after you hang up. Don't leave angry voice messages. Don't send angry, rude, disrespectful, obnoxious texts. That is nothing more than documentation and evidence that works against you.

They can play games for as long as it takes, but when that boy gets older, and wants to find himself, think about the treasure chest of documentation and other artifacts that you can hand to him in a box. Actual first-hand proof of your resilience and effort over the years. Save and print text messages, keep voicemails and have them transcribed. Have the calendars with the notes, keep a journal, and so on. Keep store receipts, but make copies because they wear out over time. I learned that the hard way! Truth be told, this book started this way. I had so much stuff. Receipts, pictures, audio recordings, videos and everything else. I knew that one day I may have to prove that I just didn't give up.

If you *have* been involved, but want to tighten up, good for you. Go ahead and do your thing. There is always one more story to read, one more conversation to have, one more meal to cook, one more school assignment to help with, and one more game to play.

Remember, you can be there without being there. Let your presence be more than just the disciplinarian. Make sure that you are not ruling your household with fear as opposed to love and respect. Your children should do the dishes because you have positively role modeled how to be helpful and hardworking, not because they don't want to get beaten or yelled at. Many of you dudes ruling your house through fear and intimidation get as quiet as a mouse when your supervisor punks you off in front of everybody on a regular basis at work. Get that together.

Understand what you *should* be afraid of. **You should be terrified of your son or daughter celebrating Father's Day with their mother instead of you.** That is absolute madness. You can't stand by and allow that to happen. Would you want to celebrate Mother's Day? No, because that is not your role. However, our Black women are out here playing the father role while we sit there and let it happen. That is preposterous. Then, we have the nerve to complain about being emasculated by them. We can't get along because they undermine our authority. They don't allow us to blah, blah, blah. How are you going to volunteer to play the back seat and criticize the route that she's driving to her destination? I mean, it's embarrassing. Black women celebrating Father's Day. I'm getting mad just writing that.

While they're out celebrating, you need to be worried about how she can only teach your son how to be a man from her point of view. Be fearful of him growing up and going from being dependent on his mommy to finding girlfriend to be his new mommy. Then you can watch him suffer while she goes behind his back and fools around with a "man's man" who takes the lead and handles his business because he was raised with an involved father who taught him how to hold it down.

You also ought to be terrified of your daughter learning at an early age that Black men are not dependable and should not be trusted. Think about her settling with someone who will not be there to love, help and support her. Be afraid of her winding up in the same predicament that you put her mother in and not even realizing the pattern that she is caught up in. Remember, you are setting examples. Enough of this "do as I say, not as I do" nonsense. You are a role model, intentional or not. You don't have a choice about that. The choice you have is whether you are going to be a positive or negative role model. That's it.

The bottom line is that you have to move forward. Don't look back. You can remember the past to take lessons from it, but think of teaching your son or daughter how to ride a bike. Once they get their balance on their own and you let them go, they are all good until when? The moment they look back. Crash.

STEP NINE TAKEAWAYS

1. Own your mistakes, but learn from them and move forward.

2. Accept other people's role in setbacks, but don't dwell on them.

3. Negative or positive, you are a role model to your children.

ACTIONS TO TAKE

1. Create a list of things/situations that you are afraid of.

2. Address how you will handle them if they present themselves. That way you will be prepared if they arise.

3. Collect items (pictures, videos, audio recordings, receipts) and build a treasure chest for your kids. They will want (or need) them later.

STEP TEN

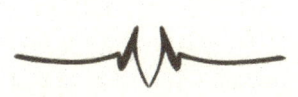

GET RID OF POLLUTION

Should I step out my shoes, give them to you?/Here's my cars and my house, you can live in that too – Nas "Hate Me Now"

Antioxidants are good for you. There are many health benefits. Antioxidants help cells fight off free radicals. See, free radicals are unpaired electrons. Electrons like to roll in two's. The free radicals are by themselves and go around looking for other electrons to link up with and cause disruption by bothering already established pairs. Essentially, they cause damage in relationships. I'm not a natural science guy. I'm a social science guy. In my world, toxic *people* cause damage. They are causing damage in your world as well. You need to eliminate these polluting relationships in your life.

This may hurt a bit, but do this exercise with me. Get your phone and open up your contacts. Scroll through slowly. You have a person in there who serves no positive purpose in your life. Hold your finger down on that person and highlight it. Keep going, you have a person in there and you can't even remember who they are. Highlight it. Keep scrolling. You have a person in there who you only talk to when you are the one reaching out. Highlight it. Keep scrolling. Find the people in there that use you. Find the people that you know you can't trust. Find the people that would not do for you what you would do for them. Find the people who don't care about your well-being while you're always concerned about theirs. Those highlighted contacts are starting to add up I see. That's crazy.

I'm not trying to be funny, but those contacts that you just deleted are not even the priorities. The ones you really need to get out of there the ones who are not growing or evolving as people. The ones that are doing the same things now that y'all were doing back in the day. The ones that have made no progress and have shown no growth. The people that don't help *you* grow. The contacts in your phone that want you to remain stagnant so that they can feel like they have the upper hand in the relationship, or at least someone to keep them company on the bottom. Watch out for these pollutants. Highlight them all and hit that delete button if you are serious about getting focused. I don't care how long you have known them. If they are being "yes men," or "yes women," they need to go. That is valuable space they are taking up, and I'm not just talking about space in your phone. I'm talking about the space in your head and the space in your life. However, if your child's mother and necessary relatives fit that description, they need a pass for obvious reasons!

You need to surround yourself with people who are already where you're trying to get to. What are you doing wasting time around a group of people where you're the most successful? So you can play top dog, huh? So you can be the big fish in a little pond? Shame on you. Now, I get that it's not all about ego and superiority. The fear of failure or fear of rejection is also lingering in there. Everybody has insecurities. Learn how to grow out of your comfort zone. Change your surroundings. I'm not saying to act like you're better than people, but don't spend so much valuable time surrounded by people that you can't learn anything from. And if you are the one who is remaining stagnant and not trying to motivate the people around you then they should definitely delete you, too. This goes both ways.

Remember that our context is fatherhood. If you have people around you that are not helping you get better, they are no benefit to your children, either. Tighten up your circle. Everybody should not have access to you like that. The less space that is taken up by useless or draining or toxic people, the more space you have for your little ones. You shouldn't even have people in your life who know you are not on good terms with your children and aren't helping, or pushing you to rectify that. People who don't want better for you will tear you down eventually. Don't wait around for that. Any extra energy and focus you have should be on making your children feel wanted, loved, and supported. Don't invest that valuable time and energy in a person or place where you know you're not getting a return. Especially if it is taking away from the kids. Remember that long-term exposure to pollution causes damaging health risks.

STEP TEN TAKEAWAYS

1. Be mindful of people around you who are keeping you away from your goals.

2. Completely avoid toxic people and environments.

ACTIONS TO TAKE

1. Do a contact list purge in your phone of people who are not good for you.

2. Surround yourself with people who are already where you want to be and learn from them.

STEP ELEVEN

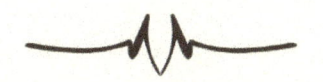

INCLUDE THE RIGHT PEOPLE

Count them blessings and pay them dues/Keep rolling with the winners, cause' they don't lose

- Large Professor "In the Sun"

Now that you eliminated pollution (a.k.a., the toxic) people from your circle, it's time to rebuild. This is where we focus on quality versus quantity. A tight circle of valuable people rather than a large circle of worthless ones.

Study successful people. Realize that successful people invest their time with other successful people. Successful people network with power players in business, finance, real estate, and so on. You chill with your "mans and them." What a difference. When a person wants to know how to start a business, they interact with and pick the brains of people who are successful in business. When a person is trying to get a job, they use people as references. If you get lost, you ask for directions. Why are you not consulting with the people that you consider to be good fathers? Use them as a reference. Pick their brains. Go on play dates. Don't be paranoid and act like that is just for women. There is nothing wrong with a couple, or group of guys going out to meet up with their children at an amusement park, the movies, to the mall, to dinner, anywhere. There is no rule that only moms can do that. If you think that it questions your manhood, then you have the wrong idea about what manhood is. Manhood is about being that foundational piece of the Black family unit. If surrounding yourself with other strong Black foundational pieces makes you feel funny, you need to re-evaluate yourself and your situation. Maybe you're not built for this. Taking care of our children as a community of brotherhood is the manliest thing we can do. And quite frankly, it needs to happen more often.

When you get these new people in your life, you will see the difference in their approach to things. For example, successful people understand that there is enough for everybody. Nobody needs to hate on you, wish ill will on you, be jealous of you, or look to sabotage you when they have their own. Only people who don't have anything feel like it takes away from them when other people have something. Your true friend with a successful career, beautiful family, and nice home wants you to have those things too because he knows that you having them doesn't threaten what he has.

He knows that there is enough success and happiness for everybody.

Control your circle. You also want to include people in your life who want to see you grow and develop. That growth and development will benefit you as a father. Again, the reason why is that you are always role modeling. Your kids are watching everything you do. They are listening to everything you say. They are watching how you move, how you speak, and who you are around. If they see their father hanging with mature, driven, educated people, they aren't going to want to hang around bums and losers when they begin to establish their circles. If you're hanging with the dudes from the block, you are normalizing that type of crowd and the extras that come along with it.

Get yourself a mentor. This is an important step in including the right people. The beauty of a mentor is that they have already been where you are, as well as where you're trying to get to. In this case, I would recommend a Black man with children just like you. In fact, use this book as a stand-in for me until we can meet in person, but find a mentor you can contact on a regular basis. I have several mentors for different areas of my life.

Think about this. Sometimes you have to start from the beginning and navigate your way to your next steps.

If you get a mentor, he can provide the opportunity to skip steps because he already knows what's there. That makes your journey more efficient. Your goal is to have the best relationship with the kids that you can. This is time-sensitive stuff here. These kids grow fast. Also, we tend to focus on how fast the kids grow and we often forget that for every year they get older, so do we. Get it done.

Additionally, change your environment. You might be thinking, "I don't even know anybody who I could learn these things from." Perhaps, but where are you? On the couch, in your man's basement drinking Henny? Yeah, you won't meet the type of people you need to meet down there. CEOs don't hang in front of the store doing nothing all day. Get out. Grab the kids and go wherever fathers are. Go to one of those bounce house places. Joint is crawling with dads. Go to community events. Community theaters. School functions. The freaking park. Don't be "too cool" to talk to other dads. We have to get out of this habit of feeling threatened or feeling like we can't be friends with other Black men if we haven't known them since we were kids. If we all have the same goal of being good dads, we have to support each other. What I noticed with other ethnic groups is that they are cool with each other until they have a reason not to be. We are not cool with each other until there is a reason to be.

Explore and try new things. Buy an Amtrak ticket and go to the nearest city for cheap. Take the ride and talk to your kids. Get out and explore a new place together. One of the best trips I took with my daughter was a train ride from Buffalo to Syracuse University to see the women's basketball team scrimmage. A whole day just me and her. The game tickets were free and the train ride was cheap. We packed food and enjoyed ourselves. Something different, fun, and inexpensive.

Find out where kids eat free. Aside from the weekends, you can probably find every day where kids eat free. Sometimes they have magicians, live music, and face painting at these places. Look online for support groups. Instead of using social media to hook up with girls all the time, use it to start a dad's group where you can plan things and get ideas about activities. Shop at different grocery stores. Go to different restaurants. If you are stuck in a rut, you have to do things differently. It doesn't make sense to follow the same pattern and routines if you are dissatisfied with your results. Keep in mind though, you don't want to go too hard! Use the daily suggestions to plan based on your schedule, but maybe choose something nice to do once a week. If you set things up that way, it can help to build that steady consistency and trust.

Children are simple. They just want to be with you. New places are exciting. New adventures create memories and build character. Buy a tent and camp out in the living room. Take your girls on daddy-daughter-dates. Make reservations, dress up, and show them how ladies should be treated so they will truly understand. Take your son on father-son hang outs. Show your them how to be gentlemen. Teach them how to respect women. Teach them to hold doors, shake hands, and tie ties.

Also, it is especially important in damaged or undeveloped relationships to listen to the kids' stories. Make eye contact with them. Look them deep in the eye and just listen. Let your son or daughter take the lead for 15 minutes. Don't get caught up in "performing" fatherhood. Instead, you want an engaging relationship. For younger children, you could even set a timer and play with them, and let them take the lead. This is called non-directive play. It does wonders for relationships. We don't usually realize how bossy and controlling we are until we let them direct the course of play. The bottom line is, just be there for them.

STEP ELEVEN TAKEAWAYS

1. Rebuild your circle with positive people.
2. Find yourself a mentor.
3. Change your surroundings.

ACTIONS TO TAKE

1. Think about the type of people that you need to be around and seek them out.

2. Look to someone who is where you want to be as a father and lean on them for guidance.

3. Change your environment by trying new things, going to new places, even taking different routes.

STEPTWELVE

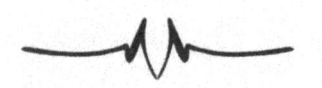

―――⌒⌒―――

PLAN AND EXECUTE

Make you all jump along to the education/Brothers gonna work it out, and stop chasing

- Chuck D *"Brothers Gonna Work it Out"*

Do what is well within your power. Take what you learned, and what you already knew. Take what you know you can do, and do it. You got this all day. Do the steps in order, every other, random, I don't care. Just get it done. Work together with the rest of us to change the trajectory of Black people. It starts with the Black fathers. It is on us. Keep in mind that you plan to fail if you fail to plan. Sit there, I mean really sit there and think about how you are going to attack this, my man. The future of our people starts here. Your children and mine need to be loved, encouraged, and taught. We owe it to them, as well as those before us.

You have already made incredible progress. You took the pledge, which was Step One. You got this far into the book. You're about done here. I told you it was light work! Find whatever you want to attack first and set up how you are going to execute it in your mind. It starts with an idea. Remember the journaling from Step Five. Write that plan out. Make it real.

Make sure to follow through. Planning is necessary, but it means nothing without execution. The beauty is that this is not a onetime plan. Take it piece by piece. If you have been away, plan and execute a reintroduction. If you are already around, plan out and execute a change in routine. Plan to get on better terms with the mother. You need each other. This is your time to put in the work that is necessary to get things to where they need to be. Kids grow up fast. You cannot get this time back. Believe me, I know. I wasted valuable years as a father, and I have caused my first-born child to be robbed out of a father. A good one. That's something I can never take back.

Here is the other thing. Be prepared for setbacks. When a boxer trains for a fight he works on defense as well as offense. He works on ducking, blocking, and counter-punching. For all the Mike Tyson clips you can find of him destroying opponents with vicious blows, you can find just as many (if not more) highlights of him evading his opponent's attacks. Train for defense. Be prepared if the initial reception is not welcoming.

Be ready for things to be going okay, and then all of a sudden, it's as if it never got better. Be ready for your child to no longer be interested. Sometimes things get a lot worse before they get better. Think of how you will keep trying after setbacks now, because giving up on your child is **NOT AN OPTION**.

I also have to add that if you have resentment towards your children, you need to dead that. That don't even sound right. Some of you don't like your children because they don't like what you like. You are offended that they don't want to be you. In one breath you're telling them to be themselves, and in the next breath you're criticizing them for finding their own way. Pick a lane dad.

Some Black fathers leave their kids hanging for all type of terrible reasons. I have seen brothers give up on their sons because they didn't abide by the often-overbearing rules of the church. Yeah, I said it. Some of y'all ought to be ashamed of yourselves treating the deacon's kids better than you treat your own. "Oh, Brother Johnson's son is a *good* young man. He sings in the choir." So? Maybe Brother Johnson would still be supportive of his son even if he wanted to paint, act, or dance. Your son could have jumped off the porch and be out in the streets being a gun boy. Yet, here you are mad that he wants to pursue something positive.

I have seen brothers lose interest in their daughters because they don't fit the mold of the type of woman they wanted them to be. They aimed to mold their daughters into new versions of the girl they had a crush on in college and it didn't work because their daughters wanted to be themselves. Some brothers want to use their children to relive their "glory" days, or most often the glory days they never had. When their children don't live up to these things, they get treated poorly. The painful thing is that some of the brothers who think that way have also experienced what that felt like from their fathers. It didn't feel good to them, but they have no qualms doing it to their children. Why would you treat your kids that way? You gotta squash that ASAP.

And all of you fathers who act funny toward your own children because you're jealous of their successes and accomplishments, you don't even get a section.

For my brothers who may be dealing with court issues, I have a strategy for you also. You may consider contacting an agency in your city to inquire about parenting classes. Many places offer services for court mandated sessions, but will also accept self-referrals. You will look real serious with a certificate from an agency stating that you put work in like that. You also get to learn a few things.

Stay focused. When things get difficult, don't let up. When things get easier, don't let up. Remember that you are playing the long game. Don't take your foot off the gas. Life is funny. We go through these role reversals. One day you will get older and need help. Wouldn't it be wonderful to have your children willing to be there for you because you were there for them? That's a beautiful thing. Your mission is to repair and strengthen your relationships, and preserve your family. You are equipped to make that happen. Now, go get those kids!

STEP TWELVE TAKEAWAYS

1. Planning is good, but following through makes the difference.

2. Be prepared for setbacks and keep pushing.

3. Giving up is not an option.

ACTIONS TO TAKE

1. Do not hold animosity toward your children.

2. Do not be jealous of your children.

3. Do not attempt to live vicariously through your children.

4. GO GET YOUR CHILDREN!!!!!!

CONCLUSION

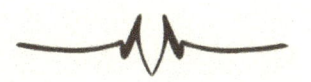

*We are **KINGS***. Let's own it. That means that our children are royalty. We must love, respect, protect, and guide them as such. We cannot expect people outside of our community to treat us better than we treat ourselves. Imagine your neighbor is an alcoholic who beats his wife on a consistent basis in front of his kids. Now imagine that dude calls the city on you for leaving your trash cans in front of the house after the garbage pickup day because you worked a double and have not been home. The nerve of that dude.

Unfortunately, that is us. We are worried about what everybody else is doing while we are destroying ourselves. We Black men have the power to change the dynamics of society as we know it. If we had a 50% increase in fathers in the home, our collective power would shift within a generation. Do you know why? It is because we would have more entrepreneurs to get some of our wealth back. We would have more teachers in our schools to teach accurate accounts of historical events and work to put a plug in the school to prison pipeline.

We would have more college graduates and career minded people. We would have fewer of our boys incarcerated.

Most importantly, we are the foundation of the Black family. Our presence alone eliminates many potential problems that we have. When we don't handle our business and play that role in our family, we invite a beast of a ripple effect. Our Black mothers can't work, or lose work because they can't find babysitters. They are leaving our children with questionable people just for convenience. They have to get help from outside sources. The list goes on. We can tighten it up. Things won't change overnight, but we can start the change and let it gain momentum. You know these teachers treat your kids differently when they know you're not involved. So do the neighbors, other kids, people at the doctor's office, and everywhere else.

Those Black children who have their fathers present are less likely to commit crimes, be arrested, get pregnant early, suffer abuse and neglect, be depressed and other things that are counterproductive to us thriving as a people. You know what prevents those things? Our visibility. So, for context, as well as transparency, I would like to provide some specific examples of how I implemented these steps in my personal life. Keep in mind that there are multiple examples for each step. These are just one quick example per step.

Step One - Take the Pledge - Long before I took this Black fatherhood pledge, I hated who I had become. I then pledged to myself that I was going to get better, be better, and become a good father. I had had enough. Doing that motivated me psychologically That is why it is the first step. Before you make changes, your mindset needs to change.

Step Two - Take Personal Responsibility - My daughter cried as she told me that she didn't understand why we weren't close. I looked her dead in her eyes and told her that it was because I was a coward. I told her that I don't want to ever hear her apologize for anything she feels that she has done wrong because she didn't do anything wrong. I did. Her actions were responses to my shortcomings as a father. I had to eat that to prevent further harm to her. A man owns up no matter how difficult or embarrassing it may be.

Step Three - Realize Your Power - I stopped going after a certain kind of woman and found out what having a real quality Black goddess is like. Never looked back. I also stepped my game up as a man so my daughters could see a good, accomplished, Black man who is attracted to a sophisticated Black woman.

Step Four - Presence over Presents - One of my daughters wanted a "Pillow Pet," so I went to the store and bought two of them. She only used one. I wasted $30.00.

I realized that overdoing it makes things less special. Then she started to look for doubles of everything she got. I created that. Then I noticed that she only talked about things we did, not things I bought. That is when I realized that it was me she cared about and appreciated, not the material stuff.

Step Five - Understand Pulchritude - During the toughest period of my life, I had a terrible self-image. I was advised to write a positive message to myself and stick it on my door-frame so I could see it every time I walked out. I thought it was a stupid idea all up until I did it, and it helped. I enjoyed seeing it. I started believing it. I began to treat myself like I mattered even when nobody else seemed to. That made me want to treat other people better. That simple thing made me recognize the beauty in my life and the world again. I became attractive to the universe. Things began to open up for me after that. That, I owe that to the man who took me in as his son when my biological father was not there, Duane Crockett.

Step Six - Stop Advertising Your Problems - One time a friend of mine called me and said "What's up man?!" I then spent about 8 minutes explaining how I was fed up, how I have been done wrong, and how I got cheated out of being a father, and how my child didn't love me, and how I try so hard, and how I should be praised, and how I'm the coolest dude, and how, how, how.

My friend said, "Yo, I will talk to you later." I later found out that he and another friend got together to hang out that night. They both agreed to have me sit that one out because I had become the downer in the crew.

Step Seven - Keep Your Promises - My daughter used to play basketball. She was really good, but was afraid of getting hit with the ball. In attempt to get rid of the fear, I thought it would be a good idea to teach her how to catch a baseball. My good friend Guy Haskins loaned me some mitts and a ball. It was so much fun! We played catch for a long time out in backyard. It was new for both of us, as I have never played baseball. We played catch a few consecutive days. She was so excited. She said, "Can we play again tomorrow?" I said, "We sure can!" She said, "You promise?" I said, "Absolutely! All we have to do is come out to the back yard!" The next day I had a very rough day at work and was exhausted. When I got home, she was all dressed and ready to go. She said "Are you ready?!" I told her, "No, maybe we can play tomorrow." She said, "Ok." A few minutes later I went into her room for something and found her balling her eyes out. I was devastated. I didn't know it was that important to her. It was the time she was looking forward to. She was probably thinking about it all day at school and couldn't wait for me to get home.

"I made up a story and said, "Hey, I was coming to see if you still wanted to play catch!" She perked up right away and we went outside. She was so excited that she launched the ball and broke my damn back porch window! I never got it fixed. It is a reminder.

Step Eight - Practice Self-Care - After suffering depression over the broken relationship with my child, I figured out that the little things would help me to come back. I began to treat myself as if I mattered again. Eating right, exercising, and taking time for myself put me in the mindset of wanting to get myself together. Nothing would have changed without that start.

Step Nine - Let Go of the Past - I almost lost the love of my life. I told her I didn't want to have any more kids because my grandfather was a terrible father, my father was a terrible father, and I was a terrible father. She didn't have kids at the time. It was a deal breaker for her. If I didn't get myself together and move on, I would have lost the best thing that ever happened to me. I almost let my past ruin my future.

Step Ten - Get Rid of Pollution - My friend said that he was struggling. Even though I was also struggling, I loaned him the little bit of money I had. He dragged on paying it back which was fine until I drove past his house and saw that his car had new gold rims on it.

Our definitions of "struggling" were not the same. I decided to run with like-minded people only after that.

Step Eleven - Rebuild with the Right People - My mentor Dr. Curtis Haynes Jr. once told me to hang around people who I aspire to be like. Once I did, I established connections, got job opportunities, developed a different outlook on life, set new goals, and most importantly, got tips on fatherhood from some of the best to ever do it. That was big.

Step Twelve - Plan and Execute - After being estranged from my beautiful daughter, I planned out everything that I was going to say to her, and how I was going to say it. I planned for her emotional response. I planned for my emotional response. I thought it up, wrote it out, and followed through with it. This is not a game. Because of these steps, I have all my children in my life again. I finally feel whole again. These steps are not made up. I practice what I preach in this book. I want the best for you, your children, and Black people overall.

Reclaim your visibility.

EXTRA STEP

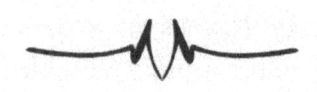

BLACK FATHERS IN JAIL AND PRISON

Go and hit the bar when the wrecks be out/Can't wait for the day when they let me out

- Styles P "Locked Up"

There is no way I could forget about you. If the Black fathers who have read this book think that they have it rough, they should consider your situation. I want you to understand that I know how you feel, brother. Although I have never been incarcerated (other than a few hours in the holding center for removing (beating down) a toxin), I have had an insider view of my uncle's experience. I have witnessed his torment as he has missed his children grow up. He even became a grandfather from the sidelines of that place.

I owe an awful lot to him for explaining to me how ridiculous I had been in the past. He couldn't talk to his kids whenever he wanted. I chose not to talk to my kids whenever I wanted. He was hours away from his kids. I was minutes from mine. He couldn't take a bus, bike, plane, train, or steps to get to his kids. I could and just didn't.

Every time I would complain about something, I was sounding like a fool. I had come to realize how insulting I was being to him for complaining. It's like when a person who makes $500,000 dollars a year complains about his current year model car's heated seats to the person who makes $28,000 a year and takes the bus. On top of that, the saddest thing that I see is when I visit him is the little kiddie area in the visitation room. It devastates me, and gets worse when they have to leave. So, I want you to think about that.

For those of you getting out soon. You have more time to plan than anybody. Plan your strategy to a tee. But make sure that part of your strategy is to refrain from contributing to the recidivism rate. That is the rate at which people get out, pick right back up where they left off on the street, and go right back in. Some of you have probably been locked up several times already. Make this your last trip. Make part of your plan fixing what you need to fix. Get treatment for your addiction. Get help for your anger. Get services to find work employment. And if I hear you went back in because you violated your terms because you smoked weed, knowing you are going to get tested, I won't be able to express the disappointment I will have in you. Is this ghetto, street, beef, hoodrat chasing life more important than being available to your kids? I hope to God it's not.

Figure out what you are going to do. If you haven't been in touch through letters and phone calls, change that. If the mother is not holding you down, accept that. Don't act like if she went in and you had the kids that you wouldn't be looking for other opportunities. If she is not bringing the kids at all, or as often as you'd like, you gotta eat that for now. If she is not giving your kids the letters, make copies. When you get out, and the kids blame you for not reaching out, hit them with a stack of dated copies as proof of your effort.

For those of you who are not getting out soon, or not getting out at all. Do what you can. Be there however you can. But don't take it personally if the kid is grown and not connected to you. Depending on how old they were when you went in, or how long you have been in, you may be more of an idea to them. It's hard to be connected to an idea. Just remain open for them. Don't make it about you. You have been inside, thinking daily about being inside. They have been out in the world thinking of and experiencing many other things. The situations are very different. Some of the things that you dwell on, they don't even consider. Be there as a support, but let them live.

Also, if they have a positive father figure in their life, don't hate that. Appreciate that. Having a good brother there eliminates a lot of the concerns mentioned earlier in this book. A Black man's presence in the home is a valuable thing. Don't let the jealousy consume you. Consider this: you have been away for a long time. You missed the milestones. He was there for them. How will the kids feel if you knock the fatherly support that they got when you were unable to provide it for them? What you're basically saying is, "If I didn't buy the food, you should starve yourself." No. Not if you truly care about them.

Brothers, if you noticed, even though this is a short read, Step Two is the longest section. That is intentional. Personal responsibility goes for you as well. In addition to what you have already read, hold this. The disparities in the criminal justice system are real, but they did not get you in there. Now, don't get me wrong. Some of you may not deserve to be there, but let's not act like some of you didn't earn your stay. The system has corruption, disparities in sentencing, unjust sentencing, and so on. But you played your part. We have to live with our choices. If you want to be better, be better. Make changes.

Handle your business.

RECLAIM YOUR VISIBILITY

ACKNOWLEDGEMENTS

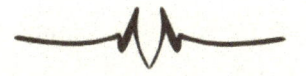

All glory to God for putting me in position to make positive contributions to the benefit of my people. Also, for allowing me to remain intact throughout the hardships in my life.

I would like to send a very sincere thank those who treated me like I was not good enough due to the way I think, look, and dress. Every time I thought about hanging it up, your desire to see me fail provided the stamina I needed to push harder. You all are amazing!

Thank you to my editor Jessica Sipos, PhD, my First Book Done Family (Connie Alleyne, Geo Derice, Roderick Jefferson, Lyna Nyamwaya, Staci Scott, Patryce Sheppard, Vania Swain), my brother André Stokes, my nephew Gabriel, and my uncle Darryl.

Thanks for the inspiration, love and support of some of the best people I know, two of the best parents in the game, my two closest/longest/dearest friends - Darnell Crockett and Felicia Stanley. Also, thanks to my mentor, Curtis Haynes Jr., PhD

A special shout out goes to my obnoxiously smoking hot wife Mrs. Hadeen Stokes and my beautiful children - Shannon, Naylani and Nayla.

And to my late father who reclaimed his visibility:

Carl Lamont Stokes Sr.